The Singing Wilderness

The Fesler-Lampert *Minnesota Heritage* Book Series

This series is published with the generous assistance of the John K. and Elsie Lampert Fesler Fund and David R. and Elizabeth P. Fesler. Its mission is to republish significant out-of-print books that contribute to our understanding and appreciation of Minnesota and the Upper Midwest.

SIGURD F. OLSON

The Singing Wilderness

ILLUSTRATIONS BY FRANCIS LEE JAQUES

University of Minnesota Press
MINNEAPOLIS

First printed in hardcover by Alfred A. Knopf, Inc., 1956.
First University of Minnesota Press edition, 1997.
Reprinted by arrangement with Alfred A. Knopf, Inc.

Published by the University of Minnesota Press
111 Third Avenue South, Suite 290
Minneapolis, MN 55401-2520

http://www.upress.umn.edu/

Printed in the United States of America on acid-free paper

Library of Congress Cataloging-in-Publication Data
Olson, Sigurd F., 1899–
The singing wilderness / Sigurd F. Olson ; illustrations by
Francis Lee Jaques. — 1st University of Minnesota Press ed.
p.   cm. —
(The Fesler-Lampert Minnesota heritage book series)
Originally published: [1st ed.]. New York : Knopf, 1956.
ISBN 978-0-8166-2992-3 (alk. paper)
1. Natural history—Minnesota—Superior National Forest.
2. Natural history—Ontario—Quetico Provincial Park.
I. Title. II. Series.
QH102.O58 1997
508.776'7—dc21   97-13328

The University of Minnesota is an equal-opportunity
educator and employer.

27 26 25 24   15 14 13 12

To

those who know and love that rugged wilderness
of rivers and lakes and forests
known as the Quetico-Superior Country

ACKNOWLEDGMENTS

I AM DEEPLY GRATEFUL FOR the help and encouragement of members of my family, especially that of Elizabeth and Vonnie; for the advice and understanding of friends who have read many of the chapters. I also wish to express my appreciation to Francis Lee Jaques for his superb portrayal of the North Country.

Certain of the chapters in this book previously appeared in magazines, occasionally under different titles. My thanks for permission to reprint them here are due to: *North Country*, *The Living Wilderness*, *Sports Illustrated*, *Gentry*, *National Parks Magazine*, *Sports Afield*, and *The Gopher Historian*.

CONTENTS

vii

CONTENTS

SUMMER

AUTUMN

WINTER

CONTENTS

The Singing Wilderness

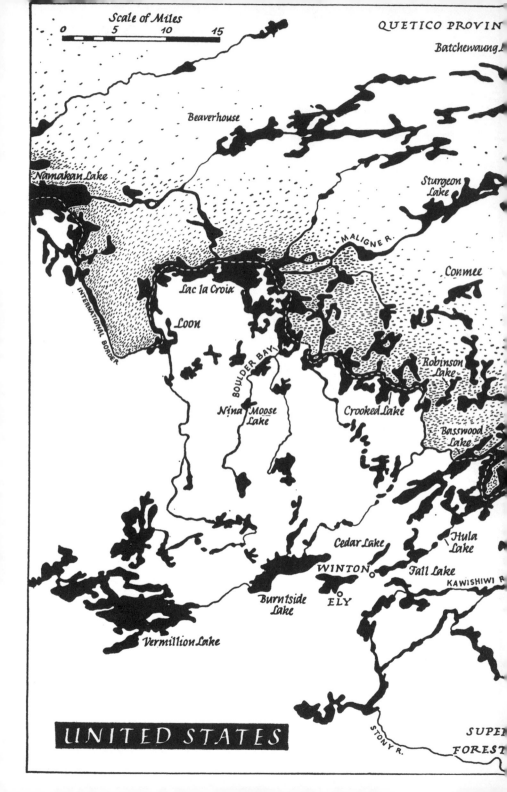

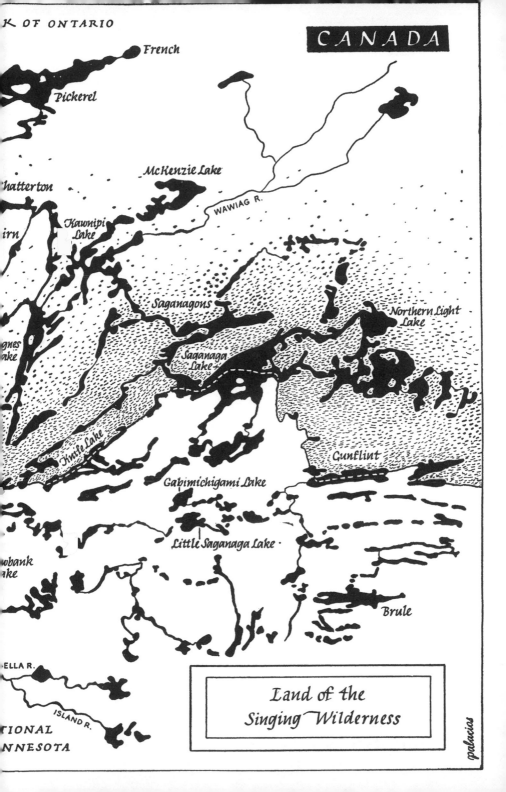

THE SINGING WILDERNESS

THE singing wilderness has to do with the calling of the loons, northern lights, and the great silences of a land lying northwest of Lake Superior. It is concerned with the simple joys, the timelessness and perspective found in a way of life that is close to the past. I have heard the singing in many places, but I seem to hear it best in the

5

wilderness lake country of the Quetico-Superior, where travel is still by pack and canoe over the ancient trails of the Indians and voyageurs.

I have heard it on misty migration nights when the dark has been alive with the high calling of birds, and in rapids when the air has been full of their rushing thunder. I have caught it at dawn when the mists were moving out of the bays, and on cold winter nights when the stars seemed close enough to touch. But the music can even be heard in the soft guttering of an open fire or in the beat of rain on a tent, and sometimes not until long afterward when, like an echo out of the past, you know it was there in some quiet place or when you were doing some simple thing in the out-of-doors.

I have discovered that I am not alone in my listening; that almost everyone is listening for something, that the search for places where the singing may be heard goes on everywhere. It seems to be part of the hunger that all of us have for a time when we were closer to lakes and rivers, to mountains and meadows and forests, than we are today. Because of our almost forgotten past there is a restlessness within us, an impatience with things as they are, which modern life with its comforts and distractions does not seem to satisfy. We sense intuitively that there must be something more, search for panaceas we hope will give us a sense of reality, fill our days and nights with such activity and our minds with such busyness that there is little time to think. When the pace stops we are often lost, and we plunge once more into the maelstrom hoping that if we move fast enough, somehow we may fill the void within us. We may not know exactly what it is we are listening for, but we hunt as instinctively for opportunities and places to listen as sick animals look for healing herbs.

Even the search is rewarding, for somehow in the process we tap the deep wells of racial experience that gives us a feeling of being part of an existence where life was simple and satisfactions were real. Uncounted centuries of the primitive have left their mark upon us, and civilization has not changed emotional needs that were ours before the dawn of history. That is the reason for the hunger, the listening, and the constant search. Should we actually glimpse the ancient glory or hear the singing wilderness, cities and their confusion become places of quiet, speed and turmoil are slowed to the pace of the seasons, and tensions are replaced with calm.

I remember vividly the first time I heard the music. It was near the tip of a bold peninsula that reached far out into Lake Michigan, and though I was only seven at the time and knew nothing of the need of solitude, or the hunger I have known since, the response was there. The moan of foghorns and the deep-throated whistles of lake boats were part of my childhood dreams. We lived inland, and I used to lie awake at night and listen to them far out in the dark and wonder at the mystery of the night that engulfed them.

The time came when I felt I must go to the lake through the forest that lay between, see for myself the open reaches of water, the ships whose voices I had heard, the waves and cliffs of the coast. One day, all alone, I started out through woods I had never traversed. At that time there were lynx and wildcats there and I had heard gruesome stories of how they lay in wait to pounce on wanderers passing through. I ran most of the long, winding trail, and when I burst at last out of the gloom I was frightened and breathless. Before me were space and a sparkling blue horizon, with no land as far as I could see. An abandoned pier reached out from the shore and I picked my way over the huge blocks of stone to its very end. There I found a deep well of clear water down between them.

A school of perch darted in and out of the rocks. They were green and gold and black, and I was fascinated by their beauty. Seagulls wheeled and cried above me. Waves crashed against the pier. I was alone in a wild and lovely place, part at last of the wind and the water, part of the dark forest through which I had come, and of all the wild sounds and colors and feelings of the place I had found. That day I entered into a life of indescribable beauty and delight. There I believe I heard the singing wilderness for the first time.

I kept the pier a secret and stole away there as often as I could. It was the answer to all of my childish desires, a place of magic and wonder which belonged to me alone. My perceptions were uncluttered, my impressions were pure and uninfluenced, my feelings of closeness to nature and of sympathy with creatures of the wild were true feelings. In them, I know now, was that ancient realization of oneness so hard to know or recognize as life becomes more involved. John Masefield, in speaking of his own first contact with what he called the greater life, said: "I believe that life to be the source of all that is of glory and goodness in this world and modern man not knowing that life is dwelling in death."

Some years later I discovered a stand of virgin forest known as the Northwest Corner. Here were tremendous trees, the last of the old primeval stand, and on the ground huge moss-covered logs soft and spongy with decay. This spot was different from any other I had known, even more mysterious than the pier on Lake Michigan. I used to tiptoe into that timber and creep stealthily from bole to bole, thrilled with strange and indefinable sensations, some of fear and some of wonder and delight. Those ancient trees, the green-gold twilight among them, the silence of that cushioned place did something to my boyish soul which I have never forgotten.

Another time I found a spring hole at the headwaters of a little river I knew. A shelf of rock overlooked the pool, and from it I could look down into deep, crystal-clear water. Around it stood tall trees, and at one end was a little sand beach where a trickle of a creek came in from the bog above. It was quiet there and the shadowed pool was smooth and unruffled. A school of speckled trout lay just below me, and when I tossed a pine cone onto the surface, they rose as one and the pool became alive with their splashing. That pool, the rising trout, the silence there were a bit of primitive America, untouched and unseen except by me. There, too, I heard the singing wilderness.

The first of such experiences, they were the forerunners of countless others and gave me a desire that has led me into the wilderness regions of the continent in the hope that I might hear the singing again. Since those early days I have known the mountains of the east and west, the cypress swamps and savannas of the south, the muskegs of the north. Always there has been the search and the listening, not only for me but for those who have been with me, and I have found that whenever I have renewed in even the slightest way the early sense of communion and belonging I knew as a child, whenever I have glimpsed if only for an instant the glory I knew then, happiness and joy have been mine.

In the chapters that follow, I tell of my experiences in the north, but far more important than the places I have seen or what I have done or thought about is the possibility of hearing the singing wilderness and catching perhaps its real meaning. You may not hear it exactly as I did, but somewhere along the trails I have followed, you too may know the glory.

SPRING

CHAPTER I

THE WINDS OF MARCH

To ANYONE who has spent a winter in the north and known the depths to which the snow can reach, known the weeks when the mercury stays below zero, the first hint of spring is a major event. You must live in the north to understand it. You cannot just come up for it as you might go to Florida for the sunshine and the surf. To appreciate it, you must wait for it a long time, hope and dream about it, and go through considerable enduring.

Looking forward to spring plays the same part in morale-building in the north as rumors do in an army camp. The very thought of it is something to live for when the days are bitter and winter is stretching out a little longer than it should. When March comes in, no matter how cold and blustery it is, the time is ripe for signs.

It makes no difference if the ice is still thick on the lakes and the drifts are as deep as ever. When that something is in the wind, the entire situation is changed. I caught it one day toward the end of March, just the faintest hint of softness in the air, a slight tempering of the cold, a promise that hadn't been there before. I forgot my work and all immediate responsibilities and went out of doors. On the sunny side of the house I stood and looked and waited, expecting something to happen, but the drifts were the same and the wind out of the northwest was not different from the gales that had piled the snows for the past months. Then I became conscious of the sound of trickling water beside me—nothing more than a whisper, but the forerunner, I knew, of a million coming trickles that would take down the drifts of the entire countryside.

It was there that I got my first real whiff of spring: the smell of warming trees, pines and balsams and resins beginning to soften on the south slopes. I stood there and sniffed like a hound on the loose, winnowing through my starved nostrils the whole composite picture of coming events.

Below the house was a little patch of bare ground with a

big drift curling over it. There the March sun had really got in its work and from under the lip of the drift came an almost inaudible tinkling, the breaking down of the ice crystals that had formed when the first storms came.

Beside me was a balsam, and I took a handful of the needles and rubbed them in the palm of my hand. Now they smelled as needles should, reminding me of the wilderness with its sparkling lakes, its portages and campsites, and a thousand things that played havoc with my peace of mind. It was then I saw the squirrel sunning itself on a branch just above me. Its eyes were closed, but I knew it was aware of my slightest move, for when I shifted my position the white-edged rims opened wide. It stretched itself luxuriously, quivered in a sort of squirrelly ecstasy, loosened up as though it was undoing all the kinks and knots of its muscles.

I strolled along through the back part of the village and there against a haystack saw a couple of logging horses shaggy and unkempt from their winter in the woods. They stood, heads down, letting the full force of the sun beat upon their backs. To them this meant green pastures and warmth, the end of nights in a log shelter with the snow banked against the north wind, no more getting out at dawn at forty below to haul the creaking sleighs down the icy tote roads to the cuttings.

On a shed beside the haystack a cat was stretched out, sound asleep. As I stroked its tiger back, it arched against my hand and the soft purring changed to a vibrating rumble from deep within. It was dreaming its own cat dreams of hunting in the long grass of the meadow, of stealing through lush woods in search of young rabbits, of warm, black nights when the whole jungle of back alleys, hedges, and gardens was a tropical paradise.

I had seen enough and walked back swiftly toward the house, but when I got inside and looked at my typewriter the sun had done its work and planted the seeds of indolence in my soul. In a couple of hours I felt better because the wind turned into a swirling blizzard, the temperature began to drop, and the dream was almost forgotten. But after that first day nothing was quite the same.

It was a month later before I had a chance to steep my senses in the things I'd been thinking about. The snow was gone and the valleys and the meadows were flush with water. The first flowers were out and the hills looked as though someone had taken a great brush and stroked them gently with light green. At the edge of town I found a pond full to the brim with melted snow. Killdeer were calling from the banks and red-winged blackbirds were tuning up in the bushes around it. At the edge of the pond I lay down on a dry hummock of grass with my face close to the surface of the water. Gradually the water grew calm, reflections disappeared, and I distinguished leaves, small pebbles, bits of grass.

A brilliant red water spider crawled up and down a brown stem. Black diving beetles scuttled everywhere, their tails holding silver bubbles that gleamed like jewels. Then right beneath my eyes cruised a task force of golden crustacea, a fleet of galleons in full sail. The pond was alive with brilliant forms of life which a short month before had been buried in frozen muck. That pool of snow water was their world; a few days of life under the April sun was all they would ever know. Those dazzling golden galleons were doomed as swiftly as they were born.

Leaving the pond, I walked along an old logging road into a stand of aspen and birch, and there I heard the drumming of a partridge. I stalked the sound and saw the bird strutting up and down its drumming-log, tail spread, shoulders back until it seemed to be standing upright. Then came the slow, muffled beat of the wings increasing to a swift crescendo that had in it the booming quality of tom-toms. As I stood there and listened, I had visions of what was to come, for that sound was part of many things: trout streams in May, lakes calm in the twilight, hazy afternoons with the smell of smoke in the air, loons calling on the open water.

A little farther on, I found a trickle of a creek, the banks covered with marsh marigold—the flower of the spring floods. The earth was trying its best to cover its soggy desolation while waiting for the green of early summer. The butter-yellow mats that had come so swiftly would hold sway until other flowers began to bloom, adding a note of color and aliveness. But by the time the creeks were back to summer levels, the marigold would be forgotten, remembered only by trout fishermen as bedding in their creels.

I followed the creek for over a mile until it became a veritable torrent from the water of many swamps and slopes pouring into it. From a hill, I could see where it fanned out into a marsh-grass meadow before emptying into the lake. At this time of year the northern pike were working their way upstream to spawn in the warmer pools of the headwaters. The fish had sensed those waters far down in the icy depths of the lake, and knew that this was the time to follow them to their source.

Climbing down the hill, I stalked the creek cautiously and sat down on a bank where I could watch without being seen. Then there was a streak across the pool beside me and a thrashing in the riffles. Soon there were other shadows in the pool and the riffle became alive. Farther downstream in another pool were a dozen pike awaiting the strength to throw themselves up and over the rocks directly above. While I stood there they began, and in a moment the little gorge was churned white with their fighting to get into the pool above them. Clear out of the water they threw themselves, and several were injured on the jagged projecting rocks of the bank. Eventually all worked their way over the obstructions and the riffle was quiet once more.

Below this spot was a grassy meadow, and there I found them swimming around the tussocks of grass, depositing their eggs in water that was no more than a few inches deep, unaware that in a few days the creek might be down and the precious eggs left high and dry. Some would survive, but hundreds of thousands would perish. The chance was worth while, for these waters were warm and there were few enemies and no storms or turbulence. Like the salmon, the shad, and the trout, they were obeying the irresistible impulse to return to old spawning-grounds to fulfill their destiny. The pike swimming around in the long grass of the meadow were completing the age-old cycle.

As I walked back toward home, the grouse was drumming on its log and the frogs were tuning up in the little pond. The killdeer were quiet now and the blackbirds had gone to sleep, but I heard the song of the hermit thrush, the clear violin notes that in a little while would make every valley alive with music. Spring in the north was worth waiting for and dreaming about for half the year.

CHAPTER 2

NO PLACE BETWEEN

To the Chippewas that sprawling series of lakes and rivers known as the Kawashaway was a land of mystery. Bounded by brooding stands of pine, its waters were dark, their origins unknown. According to the ancients, the land belonged to those who had gone, was forbidden to those who lived. From the Algonquin *Kaw* meaning "no" and *Ashaway* meaning "the place between," it took its name: "no place between," a spirit land.

Primitive races all over the world have such places, their origins buried in mystery and forgotten legends. Strange things have happened there, and the sense of awe and mystery is always present. The terrain is colored by it, as is everything found there. Some of the old ones understand and know why this must be, but the young ones laugh and ignore the taboos of the past.

I chose the Kawashaway, now known as Kawishiwi, for the most important expedition of the year, the time when the snow was gone from the ice and the waters from its melting had drained through fissures into the depths below. It was the time when the wilderness of the forbidden land was as alone as it used to be. I wanted to have it to myself so that when I was deep within it I might discover some of the secret of the Chippewas, sense some of the ancient mystery surrounding it. If I did not find what I sought, I still would know the beauty of the country at the time of awakening, when there was a softness in the wind and the long-frozen land was breathing again, expanding and stirring with life after months of rigid immobility.

Daylight of a morning in April found me at Silver Rapids, where the waters of White Iron Lake tumbled into the north Kawishiwi. For a quarter-mile there was open water, a long blue gash of it eating its way into the ice. Where it finally ran underneath, there was a rending and lifting that was slowly breaking the main mass on the river. I was afoot, alone, yet there was little danger if one watched the holes and fissures and used care in getting across the open water that now separated the ice from the shore. Only along the paths of the summer portages was the snow still deep. Even here in the mornings before the sun was high the crust was hard enough to walk upon.

Before me stretched twenty miles of brittle frozen surface. My pack rode lightly and the crust was rough enough for perfect footing. What a contrast to the slow, plodding steps of snowshoes! This was sheer joy in movement, and I reached for the clear, open miles ahead.

Gradually the streamers of rose and mauve in the east changed to gold, and then the sun burst over a spruce-etched hill. At that moment the river was transformed into a brilliant crystalline boulevard stretching to infinity. The air was mountain air that morning, and my feet were winged. I was in the forbidden land, land of the spirits, a place to approach with awe and perhaps with prayer.

Within an hour I could see the notch in the hills which marked the first portage. I passed between islands thickly wooded with jack pine and spruce, threaded a narrows choked with the gaunt silver spires of cedar killed by high water, then approached Dead Man's Rapids. I could hear the roar of plunging water long before I could see it. Years before, a lumberjack had been killed there, breaking a log jam. Below was a widening pool with the current gnawing into the blackening fringe of ice along its edges. As I approached, a flock of goldeneyes took to the air and circled widely. The whistling of their wings was a new and pleasant sound. Then they returned and landed with a confident splash in the very spot from which they had flown.

I skirted the weak ice carefully, jumped a moat of open water near the shore, and was on high ground. A few paces back from the rocks, the snow was still deep but frozen so hard I could walk on top. At the other end of the portage I found a huge pyramidal block of ledge, Haystack Rock, stranded in midchannel by the glacial ice. Two more detours around open water and I was again on a stretch of frozen river just this side of the long carry known as Murphy's Portage. How incongruous those names: Dead Man's Portage, Murphy's, Haystack Rock, names of a violent era just passed, axes and peaveys, spiked boots and river pigs, far cry from the sacred ground, the spirit land of the Chippewas.

Now the shores were bold walls of rock, barren, burned over, and desolate. The south shore was still frozen and white, but the north, exposed like a sloping hotbed to the sun, was brown and dry. The leaves and duff looked good to me. I wanted to burrow into the crumbling dark humus underneath, feel it, smell it, and steep myself in its warmth. There was a long stretch of shore without a trace of snow from the edge of the ice to the skyline.

As I worked my way close, the brush cracked and a deer scampered up the slope. Three more joined it, their white flags bouncing and floating over the windfalls. For them that strip of brown earth was a reprieve, a reward for survival. No more deep-frozen trails in the deeryards, no more desperate reaching for cedar twigs, no more starvation at forty below. Farther on I startled a buck and a doe. The buck snorted, wheeled, and sped for the cliffs. Twenty feet at a time, he literally soared over rocks and logs, and scaled slippery ice-rimmed slopes with the reckless and sure-footed abandon of a mountain goat. Suddenly there were flashing tails everywhere and then a bold silhouette of the herd against the blue of the sky. During the next few miles I was never out of sight of deer. They had come great distances to feed on that first bare strip along the north shore of the Kawishiwi.

The river now tumbled through a narrow, rocky canyon. Flush and churning golden-brown, it bored its way through gorges and dells, swirled in foam-laced whirlpools, and fought the windfalls and debris of the spring before. Then I was out in the main channel, hiking through a labyrinth of spruce-fringed islands and indentations.

A raven flew high above me, circled and circled, watching the lone black figure down on the ice. That crumbling highway was worth watching this time of year. A short time before, I had seen a deer plunge straight across the narrows, miss the holes and cracks with its slender pipestem legs, and hit the blue water strip near shore in a sparkling flash of spray. I knew the raven had seen it too and the jumps I made as well. The forbidden land was good hunting in the spring.

On the long portage between the river and Snowbank Lake, I found the first hard going. It was late afternoon when I reached it, and the sun had softened the crust. To make things worse, two moose had stumbled and plunged down the full length of it, pitting it with great uneven holes. Then the shadows lengthened and it was hard to tell which was shadow and which was hole. The two miles were long, and when I burst through the last clump of jack pine, it was dark. There was no moon, but the blue-black dome of the sky was bright with stars. The Great Bear hung low, and Cassiopeia and the Pleiades seemed close enough to touch. Ahead was open space for miles. Beyond that, Knife, the Quetico, the roaring Saganagons.

I sat there and rested for a long time. A chorus of coyote howls came from the hills of Lake Disappointment across the bay, and an owl hooted back in the timber. Was there meaning in the Indian paintings on the cliffs east of Insula, in the naming of the Manitou River just over the divide toward Lake Superior? The legends were buried with the last of the old Chippewas. I wondered if I would ever know the spirit land. All I could do was be aware, try to catch something of the sense of awe which once was theirs.

There was movement on the lake, an uneasy whispering, a shoving and a flexing, and ominous groans came from the darkness ahead. I decided not to head out onto the ice, but to follow the shore closely to the trapper's cabin a mile beyond. With a long pole, I moved cautiously onto the ice and slid the point ahead, feeling out the cracks and soft places. In half an hour I was there. The little shelter back in the spruces was still buried in snow and the door covered with drift. A deep, well-beaten, narrow trail led under one corner, and when I saw the board that had been gnawed I knew a porcupine was inside. As I stepped within, it chattered its teeth in the dark beneath the bunk. Then, gathering courage, it waddled past me out into the night. Candlelight and a roaring fire in the little Yukon stove, then supper, fresh boughs, and sleep.

The morning found me hiking down the smooth, wind-polished surface of the lake. In places the ice was covered with frost crystals as big as butterflies and much the same shape. Long crevices were bordered with them, and when the sunlight struck there were flashes of silver and blue and sometimes of flame. Those crystals were the frozen breath of the lake, evidence of its awakening.

A cluster of rocky islands lay to the north, with narrow channels and reefs among them. Trout spawned on those reefs in the fall, and stayed there until after the ice was gone and the water warmed. Then they moved again to the cold and constant depths of the lake and stayed until the lowering temperatures on the surface brought them once more to the shallows. In those days the season was open in April.

In the lee of an island covered with a stand of pine, I began to chop a hole and discovered that there was still almost two feet of clear blue ice. When I had finished, I went to the island, cut an armful of balsam boughs, laid them beside the hole, and baited my line with a silver smelt. It was good to lie there in the sun. I studied the shorelines, gazed at the sweep of ice, and watched the sky. Once a wolf, as leisurely as I, crossed between me and the cabin, stopped and looked my way, then disappeared behind a point of land. Ravens wheeled and turned lazily far in the blue.

Just as I hauled in my line for the hundredth time, something took hold and began to move away. I played out line—ten, twenty, thirty feet—and struck hard. The hook set firmly and the fun began—wild dashes around the hole, swirling dives to the bottom, long uncertain sulks. Then, urging the fish toward the opening, I lay with my face close to the water, watching for the flash of ghostly silver. When it came, it startled me—it was so close. The fish must have been just as startled as I, for it made a dash toward the bottom, almost tearing the line from my hand. Then it was up against the ice, five pounds of beautiful trout, enough for several days.

Summer trout from those clear waters are good to look at, but a trout in the spring is a sight to behold—gold and silver with red fins, iridescent in the sun, full-bodied, hard and icy cold as the lake itself. I cleaned it carefully beside the hole and left the head, entrails, and backbone for the waiting ravens.

That afternoon I cooked and ate it in the sunshine in front of the cabin, then spent the rest of the day reading Thoreau and making friends with a couple of Canada jays and a red squirrel. The spruces were full of the soft mating-calls of the chickadees, the sound which more than any other proves that the sun is warm on the south sides of trees, that spring is on the way. When I whistled the plaintive two-noted mating-call they grew excited, flew close to where I sat, tried to find the stranger in their midst.

One day I found a fresh bear trail and followed it back to an abandoned den beneath a windfall. Another time I followed a winding sedge-bordered creek and found where a pair of otters had been running and sliding along it, diving under the ice wherever it was broken, only to come out at a new opening for another slide. I saw a big brown beaver sunning itself on a rock close to the water's edge, found the deep furrow it had made to a clump of young aspen back from the shore. The days were full of such adventures, so full that I almost forgot about the ice and that I must leave before the blackening rivers became raging torrents and my glistening highway was gone.

One morning, an hour before dawn, I closed the door of the cabin and left the forbidden land to its crumbling ice and roaring rapids, to its dreams of mystery and of the past. I had not found the secret of the Chippewas, but I had known for a little while the ancient beauties of their solitudes, the warmth of the April sun, a glittering icy highway, and frost crystals as big as butterflies. I had seen the stars very close, had heard the song of the coyotes and listened to the first full breathing of the lake. I had made medicine with the chickadees and the whisky-jacks, had played a game of hide-and-seek with the ravens, had caught a trout and seen its ghostly flash in the blue-black depths of the lake. I had spent some days as leisurely as a bear coming out of its den, soaking up the warmth of spring.

When I thought of all the things I had done, I felt I had known a little of the awe, even some of the fear that must have been the Chippewas' in their spirit land of No Place Between.

CHAPTER 3

THE STORM

I T WAS mid-April before I heard the first robin singing as only robins can before a rain, the fluid, haunting melody of gurgling notes which sounds like the flowing of water itself. As yet the grass had not begun to green, but there had been mist, and a soft lushness had come into the air which spoke of more to come.

The snow was all but gone now; only in the deep, shaded valleys and on the north slopes was there any sign at all. Some of the smaller lakes had opened, but the larger ones were as solid as they had ever been. The ice was blackening, and at the mouths of creeks and rivers there were long blue V's of open water. The song of the robin meant many things to me: getting up early and listening to the birds; long walks through the woods to the headwaters of trout streams with the sun bursting over the tops of trees and the underbrush sparkling with dew. It meant the sharp pungence once more of the low places at dusk, the flaming of the dogwood stems along the creeks; the reddening of the maples and the bursting of their blooms long before the leaves. It meant pussy willows in every swamp, white drifts of them against the brown of the still-frozen bogs; the Nile green that would brush the poplars and, with the pearl-gray masses of the large-toothed aspen, make each hillside and valley a pastel dream.

The robin meant the end of many things—of ski trails, and rabbit tracks, and the beds of deer in the snow. Life had changed suddenly and was full of a new excitement. From that time on I was a scout and a spy, spending every waking moment anticipating the smells, sights, and sounds of coming events.

That same day I took a long walk over a field to the south of my home. The grass, now rid of snow, was matted and covered with grayish mold. Everywhere were the tunnels and the round grass houses of the meadow mice. Small pools of ice-cold water lay in every hollow, and I knew that some of them were full of larvæ and crustacea and other forms of life which until then had lain dormant in the muddy bottom. Before me was a sky-blue pool larger than the rest, a permanent pool with enough moisture during the summer so that cattails, sedges, and willows grew around its edges. Then came a sound that quickened my heart—the resonant *quack-quack-quack* of a mallard hen, the contented talk of ducks who have found good pasture. Not since October had I heard that sound, a breath out of the past which brought memories of rice beds golden in the sunlight, of flocks swooping out of the sky, and of sunsets when the long, trembling V's laced themselves against the afterglow. Then, of a sudden, three mallards took to the air—a drake and two hens—and climbed high, the sunlight catching the color of wing bars, the pearl gray of undersides, a splash of bronze. It was over in a moment, and I stood there watching as they headed into the north.

As I left the pond I heard a killdeer—*kill-dee-kill-dee-kill-deeeee*. For me, no other sound of early spring so completely catches the spirit of thawing earth and running water as this one call. Even more than the robin, more than the mallards, this wild, clear call epitomizes the break-up and the great migration wave to come. I watched a pair of them circling the pool, caught sight of them later running over the field, and always *kill-dee-kill-dee-kill-deeeee*.

Then I caught a flash of white wings high in the blue and heard the distant crying of seagulls heading north from Lake Superior. I knew where they were going. Although the big lakes were still frozen and would not be free until early May, there were open spots on the rivers and on the smaller ponds. They knew and were heading back to stake their claims on the little rocky islands that would be their nesting-places all over the Quetico-Superior.

Toward the end of April there were many birds: the white-throated and white-crowned sparrows in droves, the song sparrows, the black-headed Harris, and many others. The yard on top of the hill was full of them—chickadees, juncos, and evening grosbeaks by the score, but what really brought music to the hill were the purple finches. The feeding-stations were never without them, and at one time we counted a dozen full-colored males. There were robins and pine siskins and red-polls, and the music of all of them at dawn was something to hear. Never before had there been so many at one time during any migration period I could remember. They came in late April and stayed on, for the days were warm and the buds swelling fast. In sunny places the brownish-purple catkins of the alder hung heavy with pollen. The maple flowers flushed into crimson along the edges of the swamps, and the pussy willows turned gold with dust. In sheltered places the grass began to green, and the creeks were gurgling and full to the brim. The days continued sunny and warm, and as soon as one group of birds moved out another took its place.

Then one day in early May the sky darkened and, instead of rain, snow began to fall, lightly at first and then in huge flakes, until the brown earth was turned to white. The birds stayed on and other flocks came in, swelling their numbers, as they met the storm raging over the border country. The first day the snow covered all the food in the countryside. And still the flocks came in from the warm and rainy south just a short flight below. When the birds ran into the storm front, they stopped and joined those who had waited.

I shall never forget the morning of the second day with the snow still coming down: the sound of the singing at daybreak, the warbling of the purple finches, the mating-calls of the chickadees, the song sparrows, the robins, and the clear flute-like calls of the whitethroats all blended into one great symphony of thrilling sound while all the time the snow grew deeper and deeper.

Surely, I thought, the storm would not last. The sun would come out and it would disappear swiftly, but instead the cold grew more intense, a wind came up, and the snow came down as heavily as before. By the end of the week there was a foot of it, and the singing grew less and less noticeable. The birds sat dejectedly wherever there was shelter, and I picked up many that had died. Their feathers were sodden with the wet, and though I had placed out all the food I could find— suet for the chickadees, bread crumbs, chick feed, sunflower seeds—the birds were thin and emaciated. Now without fear, they gathered in droves around the feeding-stations, but they grew weaker and weaker, and more and more of them died as the storm continued.

Then came the grackles with their opaque eyes and long, sharp bills. I did not actually see them kill any of the smaller birds, but they did feed on those which had died and frightened those still alive. At the first flash of black wings all birds on the hilltop froze. There was no move to escape, just complete immobility as they waited for death to strike. The grackles would stay for a while, then leave as quickly as they had come. As soon as they were gone, the singing would begin once more in spite of the terror the birds had known.

The storm covered the north country with from twelve to sixteen inches of snow; millions of birds were stopped in their migration, and uncounted thousands must have died. Then the skies cleared, the sun came out, and in a week the ground was almost clear. The rivers were in flood now and the pools larger in the fields. The still-unfrozen buds went into fuller and fuller bloom and the grass turned swiftly into green to make up for the delay. The birds kept on singing and began to move off toward the north.

I remember getting up at dawn one morning after the storm was over. There again was the music, swelled by new species that had just come in. The purple finches, the grosbeaks, the whitethroats stayed longer than the rest, and their singing never ceased. The blizzard of May and all that it had brought were forgotten. Then came a day of warm rain and all the snows were washed away.

I listened to the robin in the tall aspen where I had heard it first, and it poured out its liquid trill as happily as before. A pair of brown thrashers came into the yard, as they have for many years, and sang from the top of a tall birch tree, imitating every bird in the yard and some they had heard in the south. They began their long hopping surveys, around and around the house, their cinnamon tails bobbing up and down. The house wrens moved into their old nest and announced to all strangers that the yard was theirs and theirs alone. The threat was gone, spring and its dangers past.

CHAPTER 4

THE LOONS OF LAC LA CROIX

THE loons of Lac la Croix are part of the vast solitudes, the hundreds of rocky islands, the long reaches of the lake toward the Maligne, the Snake, and the Namakon. My memory is full of their calling: in the morning when the white horses of the mists are galloping out of the bays, at midday when their long, lazy bugling is part of the calm, and at dusk when their music joins with that of the hermit thrushes and the wilderness is going to sleep.

But there is a time in the early spring—just after the ice goes out, while the rapids are roaring and the portages beside them half under water, while there are still pockets of snow on shady shores and the entire country is beginning to breathe again—when they really call. Once years ago on the open reaches of Lac la Croix, I heard them under the light of a spring moon, a wild, blending harmony that has haunted me ever since.

The calling of the loons was only one of several reasons for a trip down the Nina Moose River to Lac la Croix. I wanted to catch some lake trout in the shallows of one of the little lakes on the way in—to feel the fight of them before they had gone into the summer depths, but, more than that, to taste them beside a campfire before they had lost their flavor.

I wanted to see Running Rock again, where the Chippewa warriors tested their strength; to float beneath the painted rocks of Shortiss Island and wonder at the strange pictographs. Above all, I wanted to get the feel of the country at the break-up, to know once more the joy of a paddle in my hands and a canoe slipping along the shores. I wanted to dig my boots into the muskeg and feel the hard granite after months of skis and snowshoes and the white trails of the long winter.

It was midmorning of a day in May when we loaded our packs into the canoe and headed downstream. The river was in flood and the water extended far into the alders and willows of the great bog through which it flows, in contrast to the fall, when rocks were always close and over the sandy stretches there was barely enough depth to float the canoe. Beaver houses that had once stood high were now almost submerged, and freshly peeled twigs of aspen around them told that their occupants were abroad.

Approaching the first portage, we could hear the roar of the rapids, and we landed high above so as not to be sucked into the current. What a good feeling to throw on the packs and slog down the trail, and what a joy to see those rapids again and hear their rushing through the gorge! After several hours of the portages and winding channels of the river, we emerged at last into Nina Moose Lake.

It was there we saw the first haze of light green over the hills, the budding-out of the aspen. That was another reason for an early trip: to see those slopes in the ephemeral hours before they had begun to darken, while they were still misty and pastel. Grayish-white drifts of the large-toothed aspen and the rose of budding maple made poetry on every shore. One must be on time to see these things, for they do not wait.

At the foot of a riffle, pike and suckers were coming upstream to spawn and we could almost touch them as they nosed into the current. It would have been easy to snag one with a hook or pin one down with a forked stick as they thrashed their way over the rocky shallows to the quiet waters above.

We flushed flock after flock of mallards coming into the rice beds above Nina Moose, and I remembered September, when those beds lay golden in the afternoon light and the dusk was full of the whisper of wings. Male redwings perched on reeds and stubs, spreading their wings so that the sunlight caught their crimson epaulets. Grackles flew all around us, their harshness an off-note contrast to the liquid trilling of the rest. Swamps are always a pleasure because there is so much to see and hear, but in the spring, when they are full of sound, they come into their own. We followed the winding, sedge-bordered river beyond, and all the way it was the same—bird songs and running water and the sense of the entire country being in flood.

We navigated a narrow channel with the trees growing close, passed a rocky shelf, and there before us was Agnes Lake, its shores brushed with the same delicate greens we had seen on Nina Moose below. Here we would make our camp, but first there was a trout to catch from a little lake to the west. We paddled to a sandy beach, surprised a couple of deer walking along it, watched their white flags bouncing off through the timber. There we landed, unloaded our packs, and portaged the canoe into a river half a mile away. Another portage and we were drifting down the shore of a small clear-water lake, casting the shallows and rocky reefs with a spinner fly.

Almost immediately there was a strike, and on the light rod we had brought, the trout fought like a rainbow, up to the surface and out, back into the shallows and around the canoe —not as in summer, when they are taken only with heavy tackle from the deeps. We soon had two, a couple of pounds a piece, solid and beautifully colored with the golden browns and reddish tints of the little trout of inland waters. This was enough for the voyageurs' feast ahead.

Back in Agnes Lake, we picked up our packs and paddled to the rock campsite near the portage to the Boulder River entrance to Lac la Croix. The flat shelf was now almost flush with the high water, the fireplace almost within reach of the canoe. We landed and stood there looking over the intimate details of the camp we had left just seven months before: the smooth place under the pines, the tent poles and the pile of rocks beside them, the breakfast place, the log we had left; most of all, we gloried in the broad sweep of water to the southwest.

It was good to make camp again—get the tent up, the sleeping-bags laid out, and a fire under way. We set up the re-flector oven, made a pot of tea, prepared the trout. Never had fish been readied with such care or fried with such devotion. When they were the exact shade of golden brown, they were garnished with clusters of red wintergreen berries that had survived the snow. Hot biscuits, a pot of tea, and trout from the icy waters of early spring—who can place a price tag on anything so wonderful? This was worth the anticipation, the extra paddling, and the portages going in and out.

After supper we watched the afterglow and heard a loon for the first time—just a single, lonely, laughing call, but a hint of what might come on Lac la Croix. The stars came out and we sat by the fire watching them, breathing in the smells and the sounds of spring. A breeze came up and waves chuckled against the rocks.

We were up at dawn. The air was cool, and in the stillness little sounds seemed magnified. So still was it that we caught ourselves talking softly. It seemed a sacrilege to use the ax, the first blow against our log so sharp we thought the cliffs must break. We gathered chips and little sticks instead, found a tiny roll of birchbark and a handful of dry pine needles for tinder, laid the fire, and stood at the water's edge.

In the east was a blush of color, and at the mouth of the Nina Moose River a slight movement, an almost imperceptible rising of the mist. A flock of mallards went by on their way to the rice beds. A white-throated sparrow began to sing, its lone, mournful note imparting a flute-like quality to the moment. A chickadee in back of the tent called hesitantly, trying several times before it was sure.

We touched a match to the kindling, and soon the smells of early morning, the damp smells of wet rocks and duff, were joined by the richness of coffee and frying bacon. We sat close, for the air was chilly, and ate our breakfast with an eye to the east and to the mouth of the river. The horizon was brightening now, and at the mouth of the Nina Moose the mists were beginning to move, the horses becoming restive with the rising of the sun. At first they were gray and moved slowly as though afraid to start, but as the east exploded and the level shafts of light hit them, manes flashed silver and they began to run, to crowd one another, and then were in full gallop out of the river toward the expanse of open water.

I had seen them once on the Caribou when sleeping on the flat rock near the outlet. That morning they galloped through the maze of islands to the south. A year before, I had seen them at Chatterton when camped at the end of the long rapids. No full view then—only their manes plunging over the white water of the upper gorge, but how they blazed when the full light of the sun burst into the valley. Then one morning on Knife, when looking down the full sweep of the lake, I watched them come out of the bays where the creeks came in, join together in a great herd, and disappear into the hills. But no place were they better than on Nina Moose. There we could watch them from the start and follow them until they were lost among the trees or ran north toward the open range of Lac la Croix.

We broke camp and shortly afterward made the portage across the swampy trail that leads to the Boulder River. We shot a small riffle that we had portaged the summer before, and then were cruising through a magnificent stand of red and white pine. Old when the voyageurs came through, it must have looked to them as it did to us—the tall, straight trunks close to the water's edge, the tops a solid bank against the sky.

On the ridge of a narrow peninsula at the base of Boulder Bay where the river empties into Lac la Croix, we went ashore and walked on the clean, deep carpet of needles. Here was a stand as perfect as any we had seen. At one time a trapper's cabin had been there, a low little structure built of straight logs, its wide eaves close to the duff. Somehow it had seemed a part of that scene, its quiet serenity part of the tall, smooth trunks and the silences of Boulder Bay. I knew Chris Talle, who had once lived there, and knew too the love he had for

44

those pines and for his view down the great waterway of Lac la Croix.

We paddled out to the mouth of the bay, from which we could see the open reaches of the lake. The great surfaces of Running Rock were alive with movement, glittering with thousands of rivulets that spread fanlike over the granite slopes, caught the light, and lost it when they ran over the mosses and lichens and into the crevices. In the old days, so say the Chippewas, young braves started at the water's edge, raced clear to the top a thousand yards or more away, turned there, and ran back to their canoes.

We pitched our camp on a flat glaciated island facing the painted rocks. After supper we paddled to the cliff and sat there studying the Indian paintings: the imprints of hands, the moose, the war canoes, the suns and moons. You find these pictographs in the Quetico-Superior country on smooth vertical surfaces of rock along some of the major routes of travel. The reddish-brown pigment used was a mixture of iron oxide and fish oil, but who did them or when they were done no one seems to know. I like to believe that those paintings were records of exploits of the past, of heroic adventures on the warpath or on hunting-expeditions, that those who were allowed to dip their hands in the pigment and leave their imprints on the rock were those who had covered themselves with glory.

That night it was still, and in the moonlight the loons began as I had heard them before, first the wild, excited calling of a group of birds dashing across the water, then answers from other groups until the entire expanse of the lake was full of their music. We sat around until long after dark and listened, but instead of becoming quiet as the moon went high, the calling increased and there again was the wild harmony, the music that comes only once a year, when it is spring on Lac la Croix.

CHAPTER 5

BIRTHDAY ON THE MANITOU

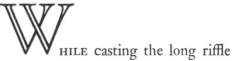

WHILE casting the long riffle below the pool, I became aware that I was not alone, that someone was there on the river with me. It wasn't that I actually heard anything, just a vague realization. I stopped and listened, but could hear nothing—only the plaintive calling of a whitethroat and the gurgling of the current beneath the alders.

I began to cast again and hooked a ten-incher from behind a boulder in midstream. Then I heard the soft unmistakable swish of a rod. It came from upstream, at the head of the big pool. There was no doubt now: swish—swish—swish, the sound of a man getting out his line. I waded out of the river and moved up toward the sound, and suddenly the joy of the morning was gone.

For years I had been coming to the headwaters of the Manitou over as rough and rugged a trail as there is along the north shore of Lake Superior: windfalls and tangled jungles of hazel brush, rocks and muskeg, black flies and mosquitoes. But because the river was mine alone when I got there, it had always been worth the effort. But now the sparkle was gone. I knew I was selfish to feel as I did about the Manitou. It was not mine any more than anyone else's, but I had always felt a certain kind of ownership there based on the fact that I had earned the right to enjoy it.

I climbed a little knoll above the big pool where I could watch without being detected. A stranger was casting a rise toward the far end. He was a small man, a spare little figure standing knee deep exactly where I used to stand at the point where the upstream riffle enters the pool. He was working the bank as though he had been there many times before and knew where to place his fly. His legs were braced and he made each cast as if afraid the force of it might throw him off balance. He was old, I could see that, far too old to be fighting the fast, treacherous waters and slippery boulders of the Manitou. I saw him take a little trout and tremble with the effort of landing it, then a larger one. He waded cautiously back toward the shallows, slipped and almost fell when he stooped to use his net.

As yet he had not seen me and I had made no sound. A trout was rising again in the far end of the pool and he was trying hard to reach it. And then I began to wonder how he had come in and what it must have taken for the old man to negotiate that long trail.

As I watched, my resentment began to leave and I knew that, whatever the reason for his coming in, it must have been very important. Far better to share the river with someone who felt as I did, and I began to look with a certain approval at the way he blended into his background, at his weather-beaten coat, the ancient, patched-up creel, the torn hatband with its fringe of flies. He was part of the rocks and trees and the music of running water.

He was casting carefully once more, and so absorbed was he that he never once looked up toward where I stood. The fine leader soared above the pool, and each time it unfurled, a trout at the far end would break water and slap the fly with its tail. For a few moments he studied the surface, then reached down and picked up a fly eddying near him. After examining it intently, he thumbed slowly through his book. Selecting a new fly, he tied it on and began casting once more. This time the trout arched above it and the old man struck. The fish was on—not a large one, but he played it as carefully as though it weighed three pounds. Never wasting a motion, he anticipated every rush. At last the trout circled slowly at his feet. As he reached with his net, he looked up and saw me.

There was no surprise, just a smile and a nod as though he had known I was there all the time. There were fine wrinkles at the corners of his eyes, and in them was the happy look of a man who was doing something he wanted to do more than anything else in the world. Wading slowly out of the stream, he came over to where I sat.

"Hello," he said, breathing hard. "You know the Manitou, too."

"Been here many times," I answered. "Nice trout in that pool."

He opened up his creel and showed me the three he had just taken, turning them over so I could see the flame along the undersides, the crimson spots and the mottling of brown and green.

"Pretty," he said. "Worth hiking in here just to see them again."

He took off the old creel. It was laced with rawhide where the willow withes were pulling apart, was dark as willow gets through many years of use. He placed it in the shade of a mossy boulder just above the water, hung his net in a bush alongside, and stood his rod against a tree. Then he sat down on the bank beside me.

"Today is my birthday," he volunteered. "Eighty years old, and this little trip is a sort of celebration. Used to make it every year in the old days, but now it's been a long time since I came in."

He pulled out his pipe, tamped it full of tobacco, drew long and luxuriously as he settled back against a pine stump.

"Had to see the old river once more, take a crack at the old pool. Came in here the first time when I was cruising timber for one of the outfits along the north shore. You should have seen the river then, all big pine and the water so dark you couldn't see the bottom anywhere. Trout in here then, big ones, three- and four-pounders lying in all the pools and the rapids fairly alive with their jumping."

"Still some nice ones if you hit it right," I said. "Always a big one waiting in the deep end of the big pool, and when there is a hatch on, most anything can happen."

"Yes, I know," he answered, "and the river is still mighty pretty, but mostly I wanted to come in here just to remember."

A trout was rising again, a good one, and the ripples circled grandly until they hit the bank.

"Just before dusk he'll take a gray hackle, perhaps a gray with a yellow body."

But the old man wasn't listening, nor was he watching the rise. He was seeing the river as it used to be.

"Where we're sitting right now, there was a stand of pine four feet through at the butt, so thick you could barely see the sky through the tops. No brush then, not a bit of popple or hazel except in the gullies, no windfalls or blackberries either —just a smooth brown carpet of needles as far as you could see. Could drive a two-horse team anywhere through these woods."

His face was alight with his memories, and his blue eyes looked past me down the river, took in the pool, the riffles below, and a whole series of little pools for a mile downstream. I followed his gaze and for a moment it seemed as though I had never seen the Manitou before. The old stumps blackened and broken by fire and decay became great pines, and the brush-choked banks were clean and deep with centuries of duff. The water before us disappeared in perennial shadows and the stream was full to overflowing once more. Rocks that now protruded were hidden beneath the surface, and from their tops floated long streamers of waving moss. The water eddied and swirled around them, and trout lay in their wakes waiting for a fly.

Then while I watched, the vision seemed to fade and I saw again the poplar-covered banks, the bright sunlight on the water, and the old man dozing quietly beside me. He must have heard me stir, for he opened his eyes wide, smiled, and rose painfully to his feet.

"Must have been dreaming a bit," he said. "I've a feeling there's another big one waiting in that pool. Better work in there, son, and take him."

I told him that I had a partner waiting for me downstream and that I'd have to hurry or I'd miss him. As I started to leave, he strapped on his battle-worn creel and picked his way once more down to the water's edge.

"Happy birthday!" I called.

He waved his rod in salute, and I left him there casting quietly, hiked clear around the pool so I wouldn't spoil his chances with the big one at the far end. The whitethroats were singing again and high up in the sky the nighthawks were beginning to zoom. There was no wind—a perfect night for a May-fly hatch on the big pool.

CHAPTER 6

SMELL OF THE MORNING

Eᴀʀʟʏ morning in the wil-
derness is the time for smells. Before senses have become con-
taminated with common odors, while they are still aware and
receptive, is the time to go hunting. Winnow the morning air
before it is adulterated with the winds and the full blaze of
sunlight, and, no matter where you happen to be, you will
find something worth remembering.

One morning not long ago I walked down the lake trail,

listening to the sounds of spring: the flowing of water and its trickling from the rocks, the oozing, sodden sounds of newly thawing earth. Redwings were calling from the cattails, killdeer keening over the meadows, but more than the sounds that May morning were the smells of wet earth and the opening of a billion buds. More alive and vibrant, more penetrating than all the rest was the heady pungence of balm of Gilead, whose great buds filled with sticky resin were just beginning to burst their hard encasing scales, releasing odors that enriched the air for a mile around.

Following the smell to its source, a dense thicket at the very end of a shallow bay, I went into its center and steeped myself in its fragrance. When I rubbed a handful of the buds in the palm of my hand, the air was charged with its almost over-powering spice.

One of my favorites is the smell of a cranberry bog at dawn while it is still covered with mist. Muskegs have a quality that is found nowhere else, an essence compounded of the heathers, sphagnum moss, and the black acidity of peat which makes it unique among all the odors of the north. Whenever a hint of it comes to me, I see the muskegs and feel them, relive the days of cranberry-picking when the hummocks are gay with crimson fruit, the copper of them in the fall and their bright greenness in the spring.

One of the grandest smells of all is the combination of pine and spruce and balsam when you can catch the wind blowing over a thousand miles of them. If you could have smelled them as I did one morning after a rain while the trees were still wet and the rising sun was bringing out the resins, you would have had a real whiff of the north. The air coming across those rain-washed hills and valleys was steeped that morning with tonic and cleanness and healing, and I thought of a city I know where the smells are those of industry and burning and where men seldom know the joy of air that has come over miles of wild, unsettled country.

Once in that same city I walked past a lumberyard where the boards were stacked into white and yellow piles. The resinous smell of them stopped me there in the sun, and for an instant the city was gone and I was back in the wilderness. Sometimes I have got the smell in new houses before they are sealed off forever with varnish and stain. Those hints of resin in the heart of the city were like a cool breeze after the heat.

The smell of resins is part of our background, part of the woods existence of our ancestors in the pine forests of other continents. Our response to them is part of our racial awareness; our subconscious is so impregnated with them, the memories they invoke are so involved with our ancient way of life that no amount of city-dwelling removed from the out-of-doors will ever completely erase them.

Of all the resinous odors in my experience, balsam seems to have the power of awakening the most vivid memories. Perhaps it is because I have lived in a country where balsam is always found. I never walk through a stand of it without rubbing some of the needles in the palm of my hand so I can breathe in a concentrated dose. That heady smell brings memories of camps all over the wilderness lake country, of balsam beds on hundreds of little islands and rocky points.

Civilization has robbed us of much of our sensitivity to smells, has dulled our original powers of perception by too much living indoors. It has substituted the by-products of industrial combustion for the natural smells of earth and water and growing things. Primitive tribes still have the faculty of smelling the weather, but few urban dwellers can sniff the air and tell what kind of day it is going to be, let alone know what flowers are in bloom or what life may be near. Through degeneration of our sense of smell, we only partially enjoy the out-of-doors.

Smell, one of the purest of our sensory impressions, cannot be seen or heard or touched, though at times it can be tasted. It stands alone and, while it may be colored by the other senses, it is never fused to the point where it loses its identity. That is why odors, if they are pure and unmixed, bring back such vivid pictures of the past.

One night in a storm I was forced to land on a rocky shore in the full beat of the waves. It was a desperate thing to do, but there was no choice, and when I threw the canoe onto a tangle of matted brush to save it from being pounded to pieces I was assailed by a spicy sweetness that I have never forgotten: the scent of bruised sweet gale. It was so sharp and so totally unexpected that, in spite of the storm and the black and threatening shore where I was forced to camp, it is the outstanding memory of that experience.

Perhaps the most delicious of all odors is the smell of certain flowers. The trailing arbutus is one of these. The first to bloom, even before the snow is all gone, this little flower seems to be a combination of the most delicate odors of the north. Nothing that comes later can approach it in subtlety. The flowers of midsummer have a stronger, more virile smell, but in these first blooms is a hint of perfection made up of the first intimations of warming earth, melting drifts, and opening buds. It seems as though all of these are brought together in one blossom to give a foretaste of what is to come. But, again, it is in the morning that the arbutus should be smelled, before the sun has stolen its essence and the winds have blown it away.

I awoke one morning near a bed of them, a whole hillside covered with their pink and white clusters. When I made my camp I did not know about them, but when I crawled out of my tent to smell the morning I realized my good fortune. It was still that morning and the smoke of my campfire rose straight up toward the sky. The robins were singing and whitethroats sounded everywhere. I did not pick a single one, but for an hour I stayed there and enjoyed them and charged my senses with their fragrance.

The smell of the morning is an adventure, and if you can start the day by going outdoors and sniffing the air, there is always a lift to the spirit. If you practice, you may some day even reach the point where you can smell the rain or an approaching storm. But of this you may be sure: whether or not you recapture the primitive perceptions completely, you will discover many things and open up undreamed-of avenues of enjoyment.

CHAPTER 7

EASTER ON THE PRAIRIE

IT WAS Easter morning and I had come from the rocks and forests of the still-frozen north to the prairies of the west. Straight from the border country with its lingering drifts of snow in the valleys and on the north slopes, its lakes still covered with clear blue ice, I could scarcely believe that there was a place where the sun shone on everything at once and all the land was warm.

I had forgotten what the prairie was like. It seemed that Sunday morning as though I had suddenly emerged from a gloomy forest, with its twilight and limited vision, into an open glade. To eyes accustomed to ridges and trees and jagged skylines, this was a veritable seashore of distance and space. I could not escape a vague sense of apprehension at being out there in the open without the protecting cover of hills or vegetation. The first settlers must have felt that way, the scouts of the wagon trains after they had crossed the Mississippi and left the forests of the dark and bloody ground far behind them. Those far blue horizons meant danger. There was no place to hide.

I started across a wide field. I wanted to feel the prairie under my feet, smell it and hear it while it was still dewy and fresh. Seven-league boots were mine that Easter morning and it seemed as though I could cruise endlessly across the open range. Here were expanse and freedom and room to breathe, and my hemmed-in woodland years slipped quickly from me. These were the grasslands of America, the buffalo country reaching clear to the foothills of the Rockies. Back north was the closeness and brooding quiet of the pines; here a wide, open world and the air alive with the singing of thousands of birds.

A meadow lark sat on a fence post before me. It threw back its head and from its pulsating throat poured an ear-piercing medley of bubbling, joyous sound which spoke of spring and water and the lushness of the prairie. No sooner had it finished than another took its place, then a hundred more from every point of the compass, until there was one continuous melody, an unbroken symphony of sound. This was the theme song of the prairie, this the song when herds of buffalo ranged the west, when the Indians rode them down from the horizons.

There was another note, the somber cooing of the mourning doves, a resonant, muted background for the lighter music of the larks. What a strange ventriloquism was theirs! I watched one sitting on the top branch of an old cottonwood near a swale, and it seemed as though its soft, gurgling notes came not only from above but from behind and below. This was really a sound of spring, of water bubbling from the earth, flowing deep along underground channels into the sodden wetness of the marshes.

It was then I saw the ruby-crowned kinglets, old friends from the north. It was good to see them again, as quiet and shy and gentle as though they were still in the forests of pine and spruce. No brazen gladness for them, none of the whole-souled pouring-out of the larks—just a soft twittering and the reserve that characterizes so many of the small birds of the north. They, too, were enjoying the open sunshine and space, feeling perhaps somewhat as I felt, a little cautious and uncertain so far away from cover.

On the other side of the field was a pond, blue as a bit of sky against the brilliant green of the grass, one of the innumerable ponds dotting the prairie everywhere. As I approached, I saw a score or more of large white birds wading sedately in the shallows, a flock of herring gulls from the larger lakes to the east, perhaps from as far as Lake Superior three hundred miles away. They had come to feed on the crustacea with which these temporary pools were alive in the early spring. Unafraid, they continued their feeding as I came close. They were used to space, could leave in a flash, trust their wings for escape. No need of caution with them, no fear of enemies.

How clean and trim they were compared to their sometimes sooty, garbage-feeding brethren in the harbor at Duluth, how snowy their breasts, how shining black the tips of their wings! They were a part of the Easter-morning picture, dignified, immaculate, all in their Sunday best.

In a tiny pool aloof from the rest, I found a pair of mallards resplendent in their spring plumage, the male with breast of bronze, emerald head, and sides of pearl. How proudly he strutted through his own little patch of sky, puffing out his chest, dragging the tips of his gorgeous wings, showing his mate what a wonderful choice she had made! They were of royal blood, their attendants a flock of demure little sandpipers, busy darting flecks of tan and white dappling the fringes of their pool.

A church bell was ringing from the crossroads at the other end of the field, and then I remembered it was Easter morning. I could see the white church with its pointed steeple and the cars gathering around it. I looked down at my wet and muddy boots, at my worn jacket. Perhaps they would not mind. I hurried over the field, climbed through a fence, startled a cock pheasant out of hiding and spent a precious moment watching it stroll unruffled before me and then, when in the cover of the hedgerow, streak as though life itself was in the balance, all dignity and poise until that last desperate run.

The churchyard was already full of cars, many of them spattered with black gumbo from the side roads, those from the farms along the blacktop shiny and clean. Men and older boys stood around uncomfortably in their Sunday clothes and talked of tractors, plowing, the price of wheat and cattle. The women and girls had gone in and were arranging Easter lilies and geraniums from many a kitchen window. I felt out of place in my outdoor clothes. Like the kinglets, I was a stranger, a migrant going through.

It was time to go in, and the men moved toward the wide, open doorway. As we crossed the threshold, I stepped into the cleanest, most scrubbed little church I had ever seen. The floor, the benches, the windows shone, and flowers were everywhere, around the pulpit and on every windowsill; this interior was as lovely as the pool with the gulls, the mallards, and the sandpipers, the lushness of the fields. Here was no musty unused building, open once a week or a month. This was part of the out-of-doors.

The little groups were quiet now—no whispering or frivolity in the house of God. Then through the open windows I heard again the chorus of the larks and from somewhere near by the deep, liquid undertones of the mourning doves. There was a breeze and the smell of a thousand miles of prairie came through the windows, fused with the sweetness of the lilies, the sharp pungence of the geraniums.

The organist was playing the somber melody of an ancient hymn, a strange contrast to the lightness without. I could hear them both, and then gradually the sounds seemed to blend one with the other and I was conscious of the melody of the larks and the undertones of the doves as a background to the majestic measures of the old song.

The pastor rose, extended his hands. Heads bowed and he began to pray.

"Our Lord and Heavenly Father, we are gathered in Thy Name to praise Thee, to ask Thy blessing this Easter morning."

The words rolled on and on, and then I heard the larks once more and knew that what he said reflected somehow the beauty and the peace of Easter on the prairie.

"May Thy goodness descend upon us; may we know Thy bounty; may we be humble in Thy presence."

Heads were still bowed, heads that had known the hopelessness of drought and powder-dry fields, the drifts of black silt along the fences, roots dead and dry in the pitiless heat and wind, wells full of dust, trees withered around their homes. Those stooping, toil-worn shoulders had known all that. They had fought and prayed and plowed their lake bottoms, and in the wet years they had drained their marshes and hurried their precious waters to the sea. They had broken the ancient sod the buffalo had known, exposed the black humus of uncounted centuries to the sun and wind. They had pioneered and tamed the west.

"May God have mercy. May His blessing descend upon us."

A gnarled brown hand gripped the top of the pew beside me. The knuckles became white, then relaxed.

"For Thou art the resurrection and the life. Amen."

Backs straightened, hands reached for the hymnals. A pretty girl tossed her blond hair and looked out the window. She caught the eye of a boy across the aisle and smiled. It was spring and Easter, not a country of dust storms, dying cattle, prelude to the desert. This morning it was the real prairie as it had been a hundred, a thousand years ago, the prairie of the wagon trains, virgin, lush, and beautiful. This morning it was Easter with the promise of resurrection and hope.

After the service was over, we were back outdoors. Youngsters laughed and shouted. There were greetings and goodbys. Cars moved to the open highway, and then I was alone. It was noon and the sun was high. The larks were quiet and the mourning doves had stopped their cooing. I could see the cars heading into the side roads toward the little islands of willow and cottonwood scattered over the prairie. It was the time for chicken dinners, apple pie, and preserves, a time for rest and visiting and forgetting the past.

CHAPTER 8

GRANDMOTHER'S TROUT

I HAVE always believed that fishing for brook trout is a spiritual thing and that those who engage in it sooner or later are touched with its magic. All trout fishermen, even the most sophisticated of the dry-fly purists, are boys at heart, with a boy's wonder and joy in a stream, the feel of it, the sounds, and the sense of being a part of its life and movement. All true trout fishermen will understand how I felt about Dead Man's Creek and the fishing I did there when Grandmother was a partner of mine and before I had ever heard of such a thing as a fly rod.

Although she had never been trout-fishing in her life, Grandmother and I had things in common: a certain sense of adventure regarding the taking of a mess of speckles, an intuitive agreement that there was nothing more important than fishing in the spring and nothing more beautiful than a speckle fresh from the creek. We knew about such matters as the smell of bursting buds and thawing earth, the calling of whippoorwills at dusk, and the afterglow of sunsets. She shared every joy that was mine, and I loved her for it as only a small boy can who has found perfect companionship. From her, I know, I inherited my feeling and love for the wild places of this earth.

Not long ago I visited Dead Man's Creek. I had come along the old trail exactly as I used to do, through the woods and around the swamps and over the clearings. It was spring and the robins were caroling and the killdeer running over the meadows. The creek was flush with melting snow, the dogwood stems were flaming in the sunshine. Yellow clintonia was in bloom, Canadian Mayflower, and in among the brown leaves peeked clusters of sky-blue hepaticas.

The creek was smaller than I remembered, and in many places I could jump across, but there were still deep, translucent pools beneath the banks, stumps and log jams, and shady places where the ground still trembled when I walked. The water was clear and cold, and under a log I caught the swift shadow of a darting trout. In those days of long ago there was no trail along the banks, for that little stream belonged only to Grandmother and to me. Although she had never seen it, she knew it well, every ripple and rock and pool, where the trout came from and how they lurked in the most impossible places.

I never knew the story of its christening, but contented my imagination with gruesome visions of lonely Indian battles, lumberjack feuds, and the adventures of the French traders who once had a post on the shores of Lake Superior where I lived.

For an hour that day I sat on the bank and remembered, reliving adventures whose vividness had never faded over the years. Below was the first pool, a somber little eddy with a Y-shaped dam of logs in its very center exactly as it used to be. I was a trout-fishing boy again, seeing the pool through a boy's eyes, hearing the music of the creek and knowing its wonder, the pure ecstasy of a world that was dewy and fresh. . . .

How darkly the water swirls between the sodden, moss-covered logs. Small sticks and bits of leaf drift down toward the swirl, then disappear in the cavernous depths beneath. I approach warily, bait my hook with the biggest, juiciest worm I can find, drop it into the head of the pool. It floats down slowly, whirls for a moment with the sticks and leaves, and then goes under the surface. The long pink worm writhes and turns, growing dimmer and dimmer as it sinks into the deep.

Then it is out of sight and there is no movement but the long streamers of moss waving in the current.

Almost imperceptibly the line tightens, moves across the pool, sinks under the log jam. I jerk the line, feel the weight of a fish, and with a wild toss heave a ten-inch speckle onto the bank. A mad scramble and it is firmly in my hands, and I sit there gloating over its color, the marvelous mottling of gray and green, the crimson spots. Still holding the trout tightly, I hunt for cowslips, picking only the finest and freshest of the big, succulent leaves. Grandmother has told me that, of all the leaves beside the creek, they keep trout the firmest. I wash bits of leaves and sand from my first fish and lay it reverently in the willow creel. How comforting to feel the twitching, the slapping of its tail! In a moment I have its mate—two ten-inchers for the feast when I return.

I follow along the stream, crawl through the brush, drop my line into every hole that may hide a trout, under logs in little swirls no bigger than my hat. Every place is a challenge, and finally I come to the big pool where the creek almost disappears beneath a pine stump. There the water is very deep below the twisted roots, deep enough to hold a monster. The worm starts down quickly, goes out of sight, and then circles slowly around in the eddy underneath. Then comes the hoped-for tightening of the line, and again I am fast to a trout. This is a bigger one than the first, and it comes out at last to thrash about on the slippery bank. I pounce upon the fish, but it slithers out of my hands; another wild splashing grab and it is gone in a flash of white through the shallows and down into the blackness beneath the stump.

The biggest trout I have ever seen on Dead Man's Creek gone forever, and I know at that searing moment such agony as I have never known before. As I sit there on the bank staring at the pool, I remember that Grandmother likes the little ones best, the ones you can eat bones and all, starting at the crisp curly tails and going right down to the head. But what a prize to have brought her, and what a story I might have told!

Wistfully I try the pool again, but this time there is no tightening of the line, and I start upstream. It is time to find a place where I can clean the fish I have taken and eat the lunch that Grandmother gave me when I started out. I soon find what I am looking for, a mossy log lying flat along the stream. Tipping out my creel, I arrange the trout according to size, wash each one carefully, and spread them out where the sun will enhance their coloring. The old leaves, now crumpled and soft, drop into the current and drift down into the ripples below. There are seven all told, the two ten-inchers and five little ones. With the sharp blade of my pocket knife I slit the silvery-white bellies, swish them tenderly back and forth in the water, lay them back in the creel on a fresh, crisp bed of cowslip leaves. They must never soften or turn color. Grandmother does not like to see the fine ribs come through the pink flesh. They must be solid, unspoiled, and sweet, just as they came from the spring waters of the creek.

Toward midafternoon, after fishing a mile upstream, I reach the spring-fed headwaters and there come to a perfect pool, dark as ebony and shaded by a huge branching spruce. It is a hard place to fish, for the bank is high, but immediately there is a flash of flame and out comes the prettiest trout of the day, dark with a crimson belly stripe, a trout sheltered from the bright rays of the sun. She will love that one, far more perhaps than the big one I lost. That one, she will tell me, is too pretty to eat.

The creek becomes smaller and smaller and soon breaks up into tiny rivulets. Fishing is over and I must head for home. I find the old trail and, with the sun setting behind me, begin the long hike back. The frogs are singing in the swamps, the robins caroling from the hills. The trail grows darker in the timber, and sometimes I stumble on roots and windfalls. Already the lowlands are sharp-scented and misty in the dusk, and I hurry along, clutching my precious creel, hoping that each hill will be my last.

Then there is a glimmer of light through the trees: the lamp in the kitchen window. I begin to run, calling as loudly as I can because I know she must be worried. The door is open, and there she stands, waiting for her adventurer to come home from the wilds. I slow to a walk, adjust my creel strap, put my hat on straight, try to appear unhurried and nonchalant. She must never know I ran.

As I step into the circle of light from the doorway, I throw open the lid of my creel. "Look, Grandmother," I shout, and hold it toward her. She takes a long look at the prize inside, sniffs the wild, sweet smell of trout fresh from the creek, helps me take them out and lay them on a white platter.

Then, while she bustles happily about, I tell her the story of each one—the two ten-inchers from the first log jam, the little ones from the eddies under the alder, the shining dark one whose spots still glow like fire in the lamplight—how they fought and how I scrambled to keep them for her. She clucks in wonderment and shakes her head in sheer admiration, goes over the entire stream with me pool by pool, rapids by rapids, listens to the birds, sees the flowers, hears the running of the water. How excited she is when I tell her of the big one underneath the stump, and how she suffers with me at the loss!

But there are more important things to do than admire trout. They are washed again under the pump outside the door, dried carefully with a clean towel, sprinkled with flour and salt, and then laid side by side in the golden sizzling butter. Tails begin to frizzle, sides change from crimson-dotted green and black to gold.

Then, under the light of the kitchen lamp, at a table spread with a new checked cloth, we sit down to a feast of trout and milk and fresh bread, an eighty-year-old lady and a boy of twelve, and talk of robins and spring and the eternal joy of fishing.

SUMMER

CHAPTER I

THE WAY OF A CANOE

THE movement of a canoe is like a reed in the wind. Silence is part of it, and the sounds of lapping water, bird songs, and wind in the trees. It is part of the medium through which it floats, the sky, the water, the shores.

A man is part of his canoe and therefore part of all it knows.

77

The instant he dips a paddle, he flows as it flows, the canoe yielding to his slightest touch, responsive to his every whim and thought. The paddle is an extension of his arm, as his arm is part of his body. Skiing down a good slope with the snow just right comes close to it, with the lightness of near-flight, the translating of even a whisper of a wish into swift action; there, too, is a sense of harmony and oneness with the earth. But to the canoeman there is nothing that compares with the joy he knows when a paddle is in his hand.

A rowboat has the fulcrum of the oarlock to control it and the energy of a man rowing is a secondary force, but in paddling the motion is direct; the fulcrum is the lower hand and wrist, and the force is transmitted without change or direction. Because of this there is correlation and control.

There is balance in the handling of a canoe, the feeling of its being a part of the bodily swing. No matter how big the waves or how the currents swirl, you are riding them as you would ride a horse, at one with its every motion. When the point is reached where the rhythm of each stroke is as poised as the movement of the canoe itself, weariness is forgotten and there is time to watch the sky and the shores without thought of distance or effort. At such a time the canoe glides along obedient to the slightest wish and paddling becomes as unconscious and automatic an effort as breathing. Should you be lucky enough to be moving across a calm surface with mirrored clouds, you may have the sensation of suspension between heaven and earth, of paddling not on the water but through the skies themselves.

If the waves are rolling and you are forced to make your way against them, there is the joy of battle, each comber an enemy to be thwarted, a problem in approach and defense. A day in the teeth of a gale—dodging from island to island, fighting one's way along the lee shore of some wind-swept point, only to dash out again into the churning water and the full force of the wind, then to do it again and again—is assurance that your sleep will be deep and your dreams profound.

There is a satisfaction in reaching some point on the map in spite of wind and weather, in keeping a rendezvous with some campsite that in the morning seemed impossible of achievement. In a canoe the battle is yours and yours alone. It is your muscle and sinew, your wit and courage against the primitive forces of the storm. That is why when after a day of battle your tent is pitched at last in the lee of some sheltering cliff, the canoe up safe and dry, and supper under way, there is an exaltation that only canoemen know.

Almost as great a challenge is running with the waves down some lake where the wind has a long unbroken sweep. Riding the rollers takes more than skill with a paddle; it takes an almost intuitive sense of the weight and size of them and a knowledge of how they will break behind you. A bad move may mean that a comber will wash the gunwales. A man must know not only his canoe and what it will do, but the meaning of the waves building up behind him. This is attack from the rear without a chance of looking back, a guessing at a power and lifting force that he cannot see. But what a fierce joy to be riding with a thousand white-maned horses racing with the wind down some wild waterway toward the blue horizons!

Rapids, too, are a challenge. Dangerous though they may be, treacherous and always unpredictable, no one who has known the canoe trails of the north does not love their thunder and the rush of them. No man who has portaged around white water, studied the swirls, the smooth, slick sweeps and the V's that point the way above the breaks, has not wondered if he should try. Rapids can be run in larger craft, in scows and rubber boats and rafts, but it is in a canoe that one really feels the river and the power of it.

Is there any suspense that quite compares with that moment of commitment when the canoe heads toward the lip of a long, roaring rapids and then is taken by its unseen power? At first there is no sense of speed, but suddenly you are part of it, involved in spume and spouting rocks. Then when there is no longer any choice and a man knows that his fate is out of hand, his is a sense of fierce abandonment when all the voyageurs of the past join the rapids in their shouting.

While the canoe is in the grip of the river, a man knows what detachment means, knows that, having entered the maelstrom, he is at its mercy until it has spent its strength. When through skill or luck he has gone through the snags, the reaching rocks, and the lunging billows, he needs no other accolade but the joy that he has known.

Only fools run rapids, say the Indians, but I know this: as

long as there are young men with the light of adventure in their eyes and a touch of wildness in their souls, rapids will be run. And when I hear tales of smashed canoes and lives as well, though I join in the chorus of condemnation of the fools who take such chances, deep in my heart I understand and bid them *bon voyage*. I have seen what happens when food and equipment are lost far from civilization and I know what it takes to traverse a wilderness where they are no trails but the waterways themselves. The elements of chance and danger are wonderful and frightening to experience and, though I bemoan the recklessness of youth, I wonder what the world would be like without it. I know it is wrong, but I am for the spirit that makes young men do the things they do. I am for the glory that they know.

But more than shooting white water, fighting the gales, or running before them is the knowledge that no part of any country is inaccessible where there are waterways with portages between them. The canoe gives a sense of unbounded range and freedom, unlimited movement and exploration such as larger craft never know. Sailboats, rowboats, launches, and cruisers are hobbled by their weight and size to the waters on which they are placed. Not so a canoe. It is as free as the wind itself, can go wherever fancy dictates. The canoeman can camp each night in a different place, explore out-of-the-way streams and their sources, find hidden corners where no one has ever been.

Wherever there are waterways, there are connecting trails

between them, portages used by primitive man for countless centuries before discovery. Although overgrown and sometimes hard to find, they are always there, and when you pack your outfit across them you are part of a great company that has passed before. When you camp on ancient campsites, those voyageurs of the past camp with you.

The feeling of being part of that tradition is one of the reasons canoemen love the sound of a paddle and the feel of it as it moves through the water. Long before the days of mechanized transportation, long before men learned to use the wheel, the waterways of the earth knew the dugout, the skin hunting-boat, the canoe. A man feels at home with a paddle in his hand, as natural and indigenous as with a bow or spear. When he swings through a stroke and the canoe moves forward, he sets in motion long-forgotten reflexes, stirs up ancient sensations deep within his subconscious.

When he has traveled for many days and is far from the settlements of his kind, when he looks over his cruising-outfit and knows it is all he owns, that he can travel with it to new country as he wills, he feels at last that he is down to the real business of living, that he has shed much that was unimportant and is in an old, polished groove of experience. Life for some strange reason has suddenly become simple and complete; his wants are few, confusion and uncertainty gone, his happiness and contentment deep.

There is magic in the feel of a paddle and the movement of a canoe, a magic compounded of distance, adventure, solitude, and peace. The way of a canoe is the way of the wilderness and of a freedom almost forgotten. It is an antidote to insecurity, the open door to waterways of ages past and a way of life with profound and abiding satisfactions. When a man is part of his canoe, he is part of all that canoes have ever known.

CHAPTER 2

MOON MAGIC

When the moon shines as it did last night, I am filled with unrest and the urge to range valleys and climb mountains. I want vistas of moonlit country from high places, must see the silver of roaring rapids and sparkling lakes. At such times I must escape houses and towns and all that is confining, be a part of the moon-drenched landscape and its continental sweep. It is only when the moon is full that I feel this way, only when it rises as it did last night, round and mellow as a great orange cheese over the horizon, slow-moving and majestic.

A quarter moon or a half or even a three-quarter moon does not do this to me, but when it is full my calm is gone and common things seem meaningless. All life is changed when the moon is full. Dogs howl madly when it comes into view and wolves make the hills resound with their wild music. Fish feed and throw themselves out of the water in sheer exuberance. Birds take to the air and sing in the glory of its light. Larger forms of game embark on galloping expeditions over their range. Under the full moon life is all adventure.

We must go back to the very beginnings of time to understand why this is so, back to the prehistoric, when the first protoplasmic droplets of life were responding to the powers of lunar attraction and the tidal cycles of the new world. The moon that moved oceans and changed the environments sheltering life in the making had a powerful and permanent effect on all protoplasm.

During the æons that followed, this influence wove itself deeply into the entire complex of animal reaction. It is not surprising that man in his era of dawning intelligence made use of lunar periods in marking time, that the moon became not only the regulator but the mentor of his activities. Man began to feel that its various phases were good or bad, as past experience indicated. More and more it became part of the dreams and mystery that shrouded his early gropings toward the meaning of life and religion. The moon worked its magic, and for untold centuries men have greeted its rising with awe and reverence.

Is it any wonder that we still marvel at the coming of each full moon, that it makes us restless, uncertain, and adventurous? Is it any wonder, even though we no longer depend on it for good or evil omens, no longer govern our lives by its appearance, that it continues to arouse strange and indefinable feelings within us? As moderns we may have forgotten its ancient meaning, but inherently our responses to moonlight are no different from those of our ancestors—or, for that matter, from the responses of all other living things on the planet. It is still an event of cosmic significance.

So, when the moon shines as it did last night, I am apt to forget my work and responsibilities and take to the open, ranging the hills beneath its magic spell, tiring myself to the point where I can lie down and sleep in the full blaze of it. For me, this is the normal thing to do, and long ago I stopped trying to curb the impulse. I am merely being true to one of the most powerful influences within me, the reaction of protoplasm to lunar force.

If humans in all their sophistication permit moonlight to affect them, how much more does it affect animals? In my own moonlit wanderings I have had abundant occasion to see what it does and how animals in the wild respond to its charm. I have listened to loons go into ecstasies on wilderness lakes, have heard them call the whole night through and dash across the water as though possessed. I have heard sleepy birds begin to sing at midnight, wolves, foxes, frogs, and owls respond to the same inherent urge.

But the most delightful expression I know is the dance of the snowshoe hare in midwinter. If when the moon is bright you station yourself near a good rabbit swamp and stay quiet, you may see it, but you will need patience and endurance, for the night must be cold and still. Soon they begin to emerge, ghostly shadows with no spot of color except the black of their eyes. Down the converging trails they come, running and chasing one another up and down the runways, cavorting crazily in the light.

If you are weary and have seen enough, make a swoosh like the sound of wings and instantly each rabbit will freeze in its tracks, waiting for death to strike. But they are not still for long. As soon as the danger is past, they begin their game again. Very seldom do they leave the safety of their runways and the protecting woods, but once last winter I found the lone track of a snowshoe rabbit several hundred yards from cover and knew that the moon had got the best of him and that under its spell he had left the woods and struck out boldly across the open field. To make sure that nothing had happened, I followed his track, expecting at any moment to see that foolish trail end with a couple of broad wingtips marking it on either side, or in a bloody snarl of fur where a dog or a prowling fox had come upon him. But the tracks went on and on, circling grandly the drifts and stone piles of the meadow. At last they headed back to the woods, but the final jumps were wide and desperate and I knew that the moon magic had worn thin. That rabbit, I concluded, must have been very young and foolish or very old and sure.

Once when camped on a rocky point along the Canadian border with the moon at full and my tent pitched in the light of it, I was lying in my sleeping-bag, tent flaps open, studying the effect of pine needles etched against the sky. Suddenly I was aware of a slight rustle as though some small animal was trying to climb the silken roof of the tent. Then I saw that it was a mouse scrambling desperately up the edge of the side wall. For a moment it hesitated, then slipped backward, and I thought it surely must fall. Another wild scramble and it was on the ridge rope itself, tottering uncertainly back and forth. Then, to my amazement, the mouse launched itself out into space and slid down the smooth and shining surface of the tent to the ground below.

The action was repeated many times until the little animal became expert and reckless and lost no time between the climb back and the sheer abandon of its slide. Faster and faster it ran, intoxicated now by its new and thrilling experience; up along the edge straight toward the center of the ridge rope, a swift leap, belly down, legs spread wide to get the full effect of the exhilarating toboggan it had found, a slide of balloon silk straight to the needle-strewn ground below.

I watched the game for a long time. Eventually I stopped trying to count the slides and wondered at last how the mouse could possibly keep up its pace. As I lay there, I became convinced that it was enjoying itself hugely, that I was witnessing an activity which had no purpose but pleasure. I had seen many animals play in the moonlight—had watched a family of otters enjoying a slide into a deep pool, beaver playing a game of tag in a pond, squirrels chasing one another wildly through the silver-splashed tops of the pines. Under the magic spell of the moon, the mouse had acted no differently than the rest.

I thought as I lay there in my bag that, if nothing else, moonlight made animals and men forget for a little while the seriousness of living; that there were moments when life could be good and play the natural outlet for energy. I knew that if a man could abandon himself as my deer mouse had done and slide down the face of the earth in the moonlight once a month —or once a year, perhaps—it would be good for his soul.

CHAPTER 3

POOLS OF THE ISABELLA

During the many years I
have fished the Isabella, it has become a part of me. I have
known many other streams, but none of them has the same
hold, the feeling of intimacy and having been lived with that
I sense on the Isabella. The Manitou, the Baptism, the Cascade,
and the Cross—I love them all, and many more clear across the

continent, but they arouse no abiding affection, no real feeling of at-homeness and belonging as does this little stream north of Lake Superior.

The Isabella is not glamorous with grand rapids, magnificent rocky pools, and big timber lining its banks. It is actually nothing but a spring-fed creek starting as a mere trickle in a cold bog, gradually growing in depth and volume until it is big enough to take a fly. The shores are often brushy, and where it has been dammed by the beaver there are muddy backwaters that can only be fished from the banks. But the water is clear and cold, and at dusk the surfaces of all its pools are rippled by rising trout.

Trout seldom grow large there. You find no two- and three-pounders as in the larger streams running into the lake, never anything more than a pound or a pound and a half, but they are wild, native speckles and as beautiful as anything in the north. Clean and firm, even the fingerlings fight viciously, and as for color, who could ever describe the iridescence, the mottling of gray and green and black, those flaming spots of crimson?

But even more than the trout are the pools themselves. Not a one but is dedicated to some memory. When I wade the Isabella, I am never alone. I always hear forgotten banter in the sounds of the rapids, the soft rhythmic swish of familiar rods. These things are as much a part of the river as the trout themselves.

Take the big pool by the rocks below the beaver dam. Dead water there and the bottom too soft to wade except where a rocky shelf slopes down to the water's edge. For a hundred yards there is no brush and a man can watch the entire surface of the pool. That place belongs to Glenn.

Glenn was an artist, and I always suspected he cared more for reflections and the way sunlight and shadows hit the pool than for the fish. He never moved far from that spot, never followed me as I thrashed through the brush and rapids of miles of stream. For hours at a time he would stand in one place casting a rise, trying fly after fly, sure that eventually some trout would take what he had to offer. Whether one did or not made little difference.

I watched him one day from across the Rock Pool. He hadn't seen me and was so absorbed at the moment that I knew he hadn't heard me either. He was casting carefully, and on his face was the supreme concentration and happiness that only trout fishermen seem to know. There was a good rise below him in a current sweeping against the alders. The trout rose again and again, and each time the fine-tapered leader unfurled directly over the spot. Once the fish rose clear, showing a broad side of flashing color. Withdrawing his fly, he stood there a long time studying the water. Finally he made his choice. This time the fly disappeared in a swirl and the trout dashed for the protection of the bank, back and forth across the pool, finally in slow, slicing circles near enough to net. A swoop, and the fish was his. He held it to the light, turned it this way and that to get the full effect of sunlight on the coloring, and slipped it almost regretfully into his creel.

At that moment he saw me and, smiling, waded across to where I stood.

"Nice work," I said. "Saw you take that last one."

He opened his creel and showed me the beauty on its bed of fern. A nice trout, to be sure, but I knew what his real catch had been that day: the reflections, the coloring, the sounds and the solitudes of which the trout was only a symbol.

The Moss Pool at the headwaters is lined by gigantic cedars underlain by a springy carpet of sphagnum. It is cool and dark there even on the warmest days, for springs bubble up beneath and the sun seldom reaches it except at high noon. That pool has a sense of the primeval, and there the world of towns and cities seems far away. It is large enough so that when you fish the lower end, the upper reaches where the rapids come foaming in are undisturbed. That pool belongs to my son. It went to him when he was very young and before he had made his mark with a fly.

One evening at the lower end I watched him casting a rise at the tip of a log just below the riffle. Broad circles spread out from the log toward the center of the pool, and for the moment my own fishing was forgotten. I was a boy again with not a thought in the world but the wonder of watching a good trout rise to a fly. That boy standing there at the upper end was me.

Suddenly there was a shout, and I jumped to my feet.

"Bring the net," he yelled, "I've got him."

I needed only a glance to know that he was fast to one of

the real trout of the Isabella. Scrambling madly over logs and windfalls and through the muskeg, I finally reached him. I waded out into the pool and, when the trout was close, slipped my net under the biggest fish either of us had seen for a long time, a squaretail fourteen inches in length, full-bodied, clean-jawed and well-colored. We stood there together, neither of us saying a word, just looking at that trout, listening to the whitethroats and the music of the rapids.

"Red Ibis," said the boy. "Took him on the way down, just like you said. Should have seen him when he broke."

His face was beaming, and in his eyes was a glory that comes only once in the lifetime of a boy, when he knows he has measured up at last.

I have been back to the Moss Pool many times since, but I never cast a line there without seeing that boy as he looked the night he caught the big one. That pool will always belong to him, and I know that when he thinks of home and of the things he used to do, that moment on the Isabella is one of his treasured memories.

The Spring Pool belongs to Elizabeth. Once after a long absence we drove out there to fish for an hour, the witching hour before dusk when there is just enough of the sunset left to make the ripples of a rising trout glow and seem alive. What happened that night burned itself so indelibly into my mind that her presence is always felt there. It was one of those perfect experiences, a combination of atmosphere, a long-dreamed-of realization come true, and appreciation by some-one who means more than anyone else in the world.

That evening we stood at the upper end of the pool just above the big triangular rock. Two trout were rising regularly between the rock and the bank. For some reason that night I wanted to show her what I really could do with a fly rod. I wanted her to catch some of the poetry and the music of an evening on the Isabella. It was terribly important just to have her there watching me and listening and seeing what happened when the fly floated down above those rising fish.

The trout surfaced regularly, sometimes one and then the other, sometimes together. A mist of gnats hovered over the water. Nighthawks zoomed high above and hermit thrushes caroled from the woods on either side. For a time I could not find the proper fly; then I changed to a tiny mosquito. The fly settled down at the edge of the nearest rise, and a broad tail washed over it. Once more and the trout came clear, arching over the fly completely, drowning it on the way down. A third cast and I heard the snap as the jaws closed. The fish was on and I felt the solid set of the hook. Underneath the lip of the rock, then swiftly toward me and the dangerous tangle of alders along the bank, a tense moment as it bored straight into them, then out into the open water. Gradually it tired, and as it flopped lazily on the surface I slipped the net underneath and held it up for Elizabeth to see.

Its mate was rising more slowly now and I knew it was tiring of the gnats still hovering over the fast-darkening pool. Waiting until the surface was dead calm, I began to cast, letting the fly float across the pool and settle as though by afterthought. When it touched, it fluttered about as though trying to shake the tiny droplets of water from its gossamer wings, then beat its way frantically across the pool. That did it, and again I felt the solid, heavy set of the hook.

But something had gone wrong. The trout was snagged underneath. Very gently I tried to urge it out, but though the line came free, I realized that the leader must have become hopelessly entangled in the brush. Dusk descended, but still the fish stayed on and I could feel it tugging steadily fully sixty feet away. There were two alternatives: wade out into the blackness of that pool, taking a chance of slipping into the depths beside the rock, or break my leader and lose all. I preferred to wade.

The water grew deeper and deeper, went over my waders, crept icily up to my armpits. Once I slipped on a round boulder and for an instant almost plunged into the depths. At last I edged toward the bank and stood there on tiptoe, trying to keep my balance and the line taut. Prayerfully I maneuvered the tip, freed the leader at last, and moved cautiously back toward the alders and away from the sloping hole. Suddenly the fish was on the surface and I netted him with a grand swoosh.

A few moments later I stood beside Elizabeth and was never prouder or happier in my life. Not large by the standards of other streams, not more than a pound or perhaps a pound and a quarter apiece, but as beautifully matched a pair of speckles as I had ever seen. What makes that evening memorable is that I took them both and that Elizabeth watched me and approved. No knight could have been more amply repaid for his feats on the field of battle than I when she looked into that creel and said: "What beauties!"

There are many other pools on the Isabella, each with its own associations and memories. Each one of those pools is like a room that has been lived in a long time. I know every rock, every log, and every riffle. That stream is home to me, and even though I am there alone, I can visit with those who have known it with me and relive their golden days as well as my own. Glenn will always be at the Rock Pool, my boy casting a rise below the riffle on the Moss, Elizabeth where she watched me that night I did the impossible and took a trout that should have got away.

CHAPTER 4

FAREWELL TO SAGANAGA

I HAD come a long way since
leaving Lac la Croix—had heard the roar of Curtain Falls,
threaded the labyrinth of islands and channels of Crooked
Lake to the painted rocks at the far east end. I had made the
historic portages around the rapids of the Basswood River and
crossed the open reaches of the lake above. Then the sweep of

Knife with its clear water and mountainous horizons, the cliffs of Ottertrack, and at last the gateway to Saganaga.

There, on the afternoon of the fifth day, I lowered my canoe into the water. The last level rays of the sunset caught a stand of dark pine on the opposite shore and brushed the trunks with flame. An exploring tentacle picked out a rocky shelf miles across the open water and made it explode with light. The lake was calm and its islands floated like battleships in a sea of crimson. Far in the distance the loons called. This was Saganaga as it used to be.

I loaded in my worn packs and pushed off toward the open sweep of the lake beyond Cache Bay. My paddle all but sang as it dipped the blue-green water, and once more came the feeling of detachment I had known when I first came in many years before. Saganaga then was deep in the wilderness, a symbol of the primitive, perfect and untouched.

Until the day when I discovered it, my life had been dominated by the search for a perfect wilderness lake. Always before me was the ideal, a place not only remote, not only of great beauty, but possessed of an intangible quality and spirit that typified to me all of the unbroken north beyond all roads. Time and again I thought I had found it, but always there was something wrong, some vague, unreasoned lack of shape or size, some totally unexplainable aspect involved with the threat of accessibility. Above all, I wanted vistas that controlled not only moonrises and sunsets, but the northern lights and the white mists of the river mouths at dawn. Sometimes it was a matter of intuition and feeling, an unsettled state of mind more than any particular physical character, that made me push on. The search drew me farther and farther into the bush, and I finally began to wonder if I actually knew what I was looking for and if I would know when I had found it.

Then one golden day I came to Saganaga. My first glimpse from the western narrows was enough, and as I stood there and looked out across the broad blue reaches to the east with their fleets of rocky islands, the hazy blue hills toward the hinterlands of the Northern Light Country, I knew I had reached my goal. How I knew without having explored the lake, I cannot say, but the instant I saw the lake, I realized it was the end of my search, and that there was nothing more beyond the hills. I shall never forget the sense of peace and joy which was mine at the discovery. Perhaps I was ready for Saganaga; perhaps all the searching that had gone before had prepared me. Whatever it was, I was content at last, knowing that I would find in this lonely solitude the realization of all my dreams.

That first experience was an ecstatic one. Each camp I made there was different from and more delightful than the one before. Even the air seemed to have a clearer, more crystalline quality than elsewhere. No two days were quite the same, and I learned to know and love the moods of the great, sprawling lake and how its winds blew and where the mists came in. I had vantage points for every great event in all kinds of weather. There was one hill from which the coyotes howled on moonlit nights and a point where the loon calls echoed for many miles around. The birds and animals around my campsites became friends, and in some of the swampy bays the moose lost their shyness when my canoe drifted in. I watched the beaver build their houses, and in a rocky bay a family of otter played around me unafraid.

In the years that followed, I came to know every island and channel, every bay and cliff. In the spring, I knew where arbutus and moccasins bloomed; in the summer, places that were white with water lilies; in the fall, where oaks and maples flamed. There was never anything lacking on Saganaga, and each time I returned, it was the same. Here at last I came to feel at home.

And then one time when I was far away I heard the news. A road had come to Saganaga. I stared in disbelief at the news-paper clipping. A road to Saganaga? It did not seem possible. The article told briefly of some new mining discovery and how a new highway would open up a vast and untouched wilderness north of Lake Superior. The very matter-of-fact-ness of the item struck me like a blow. Saganaga had come to mean far more than just another lake. It had woven itself into my consciousness, become part and parcel of all I had ever wanted, something real and true and tangible, a place secure and permanent in a world where values were always shifting and men no longer seemed to be sure of anything. I tore the little clipping into bits and crumpled them in the palm of my hand. For a long time I tried to forget, but the knowledge haunted me and I knew that some day, somehow, I must re-turn and see for myself. I must go back to the wilderness I had known.

As time went on, there was a growing compulsion about my return which could not be denied. But, knowing that Saganaga had changed, I postponed my trip year after year and contented myself with dreaming of the place I had known, the one spot in the world which for me was perfect and untouched.

Then at last I was back, and as I paddled along and saw the old familiar reaches of blue, the islands riding at anchor in the distance, the gnarled old trees and lichen-covered cliffs, it seemed as though I had never been away. As yet I had seen no change—no cabins, no motor boats—and had heard no sounds that were strange. The loons were calling as they had always called in welcome to a voyageur.

I pitched my tent under the pine trees on my old campsite, kindled my fire with dry tinder I had left there long ago. Even there I found no sign, no evidence of a change that I could only sense. As I stood at the water's edge and looked out toward the far eastern shore, the old feeling of immensity and distance came back to me, but I was apprehensive and uneasy.

That night I paddled far into the south bay through a maze of islands toward the place where I knew the road had come. There I would see for myself. Darkness gathered and the near-by shores loomed black. I paddled through channel after channel, finally emerging into the open near the mouth of a long bay where in the past I had often come to look for moose and to listen to the sounds of the night. The dark mouth of the opening widened before me and the canoe slipped silently along the shore.

I rounded a final point and there, like the rising of a full moon, was a blaze of light over the horizon, the windows of a lodge. I dropped my paddle and sat staring. I had expected exactly that and had steeled myself, but it seemed incredible and unreal. One moment the old wilderness of Saganaga, its timelessness and solitude; then in an instant, in the space of a paddle stroke, civilization and change.

From the brightly lighted lodge a broad trail of yellow ran out into the darkness. It fascinated me, and before I realized what I was doing, the canoe was gliding down its path straight into the glare. Not until I was at the very rim of the half-moon of light did I stop. In the shadows just beyond its edge I allowed the canoe to drift. Instead of the old primeval chorus, slow, seductive music trembling across the water. Strangely enough, I was not resentful at what I saw and heard. Such things had their place. But I was saddened by the realization that something had been lost, something old and beautiful and to me beyond price; that the long silence had been broken at last and that in this loved place solitude was no more.

The music stopped suddenly. The door swung wide and above the talking sounded the high, clear laughter of a girl. A group came outside. There was a flare of matches, pinpoints of light. The door opened and closed once more. Again the music and couples drifting by the windows.

Suddenly a beam of light sliced through the black of the sky, faded for an instant, then, like a meteor, burst full upon the shore, its violent brilliance eclipsing for a moment the steady yellow glow from the lodge. There was the roar of a racing motor, then quiet and blackness. The great door opened and the new arrivals were swallowed swiftly by the warmth and music within.

In a way it was very pleasant, listening and watching from the canoe. Light and music and laughter were good after days in the bush. The warmth and gaiety invited me, and suddenly in the darkness and solitude from which I had come there seemed to be a great loneliness. At that moment I doubted myself. Perhaps I had been wrong about silence and solitude, about places where time meant nothing and where a man might stand aloof and alone and listen to his dreams. Perhaps this was what it should be, this the real goal.

But then like a flood I remembered the nights I had waited and listened in this same little bay when the only sounds were the sloshing of moose in the shallows, the whack of beaver tails, the eternal song of the swamp, music that for ages past had never changed, and I knew that for me there was no question. Now there was music of a different tempo, the heady, exciting throb of drums, the tom-toms of another wilderness.

The sudden whine of an outboard motor roused me from my reverie. Out from the shore it came, straight down the path of golden light, leaping like a wild thing from wave to wave. I grasped my paddle in readiness for the swell. The boat sped by me with a shattering roar and was lost swiftly in the blackness from which I had come. The shores crashed and re-echoed with a violence of sound, but in a moment there was only the dull, monotonous drone that merged gradually with the other sounds of night. Far out toward the open lake the fierce glare of its headlight was a giant firefly dancing fitfully against the far horizon.

I swung the canoe around and began the long paddle back to the old campsite. As I pushed through the dark, winding channels, I wondered if what I had seen could really change the Saganaga the voyageurs and Chippewas had known. Did not the ancient headlands brood as calmly then as now? Did it really matter that the silence they had known was gone? Was solitude a matter of remoteness and primitive country or was it something within myself?

I half turned once more toward the brilliance of the lodge. Faintly now, softly as a caress of the south wind itself, came the strains of melody across the water. A stroke of my paddle and it was gone and the canoe was swallowed once more by the silence and darkness of the islands.

In the north toward Cache Bay the sky was bright with the shifting lights of the Aurora, the ghost dance of the past. Toward the south I had listened to strange music, a requiem to the wilderness. Although the old music was again in the night wind and in the whispering of the waves against the rocks, for me it was farewell to the Saganaga I had known.

As my canoe slipped along the shores, I knew that for them there was no change; it was not important that the silence was broken now. To them, who had seen the great ice come and go, who had watched the passing of Indian tribes and the migration of the caribou, this was but a moment in the æons they had known.

CHAPTER 5

CAMPFIRES

Something happens to a man when he sits before a fire. Strange stirrings take place within him, and a light comes into his eyes which was not there before. An open flame suddenly changes his environment to one of adventure and romance. Even an indoor fireplace has this effect, though its owner is protected by four walls and the assurance that, should the fire go out, his thermostat will keep him warm. No matter where an open fire happens to be, in a city apartment, a primitive cabin, or deep in the wilderness, it weaves its spell.

Before men ever dreamed of shelter, campfires were their homes. Here they gathered and made their first plans for communal living, for tribal hunts and raids. Here for centuries they dreamed vague dreams and became slowly aware of the first faint glimmerings and nebulous urges that eventually were to widen the gulf between them and the primitive darkness from which they sprang.

Although the gulf is wide, even now we see the future in leaping flames, making plans in their enchantment which in the brash light of day seem foolhardy. Before them, modern conquests are broached and unwritten pledges made which vary little from those of the past. Around a fire men feel that the whole world is their campsite and all men partners of the trail.

Once a man has known the warmth and companionship there, once he has tasted the thrill of stories of the chase with the firelight in his eyes, he has made contact with the past, recaptured some of the lost wonder of his early years and some of the sense of mystery of his forebears. He has reforged a link in his memory which was broken when men abandoned the life of the nomad and moved from the forests, plains, and mountains to the security of villages. Having bridged the gap, he swiftly discovers something he had lost, a sense of belonging to the earth and to his kind. When that happens, he reaches back beyond his own life experience to a time when existence was simple.

So deeply ingrained is his feeling, and all it connotes, that even the building of a fire has ritualistic significance. Whether he admits it or not, every act of preparation is vital and satisfying to civilized man. Although the fire may not be needed for warmth or protection or even the preparation of food, it is still a primal and psychological necessity. On any wilderness expedition it always serves as a climax to the adventures of the day, is as important to a complete experience as the final curtain to a play. It gives everyone an opportunity to participate in an act hallowed by the devotion of forgotten generations.

The choice of the proper spot to build a fire is important. No place is picked lightly, for there are many factors involved. From the time man first carried a living brand from some lightning-struck stub and then discovered how to generate a flame with a whirling spindle and tinder, he was set apart. He has not forgotten, and even today everyone is anxious to help the fire-builder get started. All join in the search for kindling, for resinous bits of wood and bark. How proudly each brings in his offering, what genuine satisfaction is shared when the flames take hold! As the fire burns, see how it is tended and groomed and fondled, how little chips are added as they fall away from the larger sticks, how every man polices the fringe before him and treats the blaze as the living thing it is.

Anyone who has traveled in the wilds knows how much he looks forward to the time of day when he can lay down his burden and make camp. He pictures the ideal place and all that he must find there: water, a good wood supply, protection from wind and weather. As shadows begin to lengthen, the matter of a campsite takes precedence over everything else, as it has for ages past whenever men have been on the move. The camp with its fire has always been the goal, a place worth striving toward and, once attained, worth defending against all comers.

G. M. Trevelyan once said: "We are literally children of the earth, and removed from her our spirits wither or run to various forms of insanity. Unless we can refresh ourselves at least by intermittent contact with nature, we grow awry." What he was thinking of was the need of a race of men in which ancient needs and urges are still very much alive, a race caught in the intricate and baffling milieu of a civilization that no longer provides the old satisfactions or sources of contentment.

Thoreau implied exactly the same when he said: "In wilderness is the salvation of mankind." The campfire would have typified a necessary means of contact to them both.

In years of roaming the wilds, my campfires seem like glowing beads in a long chain of experience. Some of the beads glow more than the others, and when I blow on them ever so softly, they burst into flame. When that happens, I recapture the scenes themselves, pick them out of the almost forgotten limbo of the past and make them live.

One of these glowing beads was a little camp on a bare shelf of rock beside the Isabella River. The moon was full that night and the tent was in the light of it. Because the river ran north and south at that point, the moon shone down the length of a long, silvery pool, turning the rapids at its base into a million dancing pinpoints. A whippoorwill was calling and the valley of the Isabella was full of its haunting music, a music that seemed to blend into the gurgle of the rapids, the splash of rising trout, and the sleepy calling of a white-throated sparrow disturbed by the crackling flames.

The tall spruces at the end of the pool were black against the sky, and every leaf was tinged with silver. A trout rose again and again, and widening circles moved over the pool, erasing the smooth luminescence of its surface. The campfire was part of the magic and witchery of that scene. For primitive man the night might have been tinged with superstition and perhaps with fear. We only wondered at its beauty.

One summer I made an expedition into the Maligne River country in the Quetico. We were camped on a slender spit of rock overlooking the wild, island-studded reaches of Lac la Croix. A dead pine had fallen and shattered itself on the very tip of the point, and there with chunks of the resinous wood we built our fire. We sat on a little shelf of rock under the pines where we could watch the firelight change the branches and their tracery to coppery gold. For hours we watched them and the reflection on the water, but when a loon called from the open lake and then swam like a ghost into the circle of light, the scene was touched with magic.

Another time, I was camped at the mouth of the Range River where it empties into Low Lake. The bluebills had come and gone, and a snowstorm was raging overhead. Our tent was in the shelter of a ledge that protected us from the gale. It smelled of balsam, and our sleeping-bags were dry and warm. The little campfire out in front not only meant warmth and protection from the cold, but somehow made us part of the storm. Through it we could watch the swirling snow, hear it hiss as it struck the water, see the branches of the trees and the ground becoming whiter and whiter. Once, above its whispering and the roar of the wind, we heard the sound of wings, a last belated flock hurtling down the river.

There have been countless campfires, each one different, but some so blended into their backgrounds that it is hard for them to emerge. But I have found that when I catch even a glimmer of their almost forgotten light in the eyes of some friend who has shared them with me, they begin to flame once more. Those old fires have strange and wonderful powers. Even their memories make life the adventure it was meant to be.

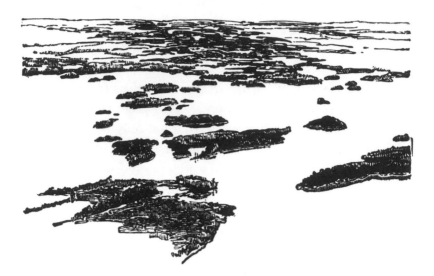

CHAPTER 6

FLYING IN

ONCE long ago I decided to fly in to a wilderness lake that for years I had reached only after many days of paddling and portaging. I wanted to see if I could recapture the old feeling of solitude and remoteness I had always known there without paying for it as I had done in the past. I wanted to know if I could get the feel of wilderness as I always used to when camped in that faraway and lovely place. It was one of my first flights and a thrilling one for me. Roaring along in a bush pilot's plane not more than a thousand feet above the trees, I felt that until then I had traveled like a mole, burrowing through the timber and brush of portages, creeping slowly down the rivers and over the wind-roughened lakes.

Now for the first time I saw the country as a whole, the hundreds of wilderness lakes I had explored. From that height I saw it as a hawk might see it: the blue and green lacework of sprawling lakes and their connecting rivers, the level lawns of muskeg, the tufted roughness of spruce and pine on the uplands. This was different from the close, intimate years when I had known the intricate maze of canoe trails as a mole might know the turnings of its runways in the turf.

To the east lay Gabemichigami, my destination; to the south the white and brawling Kawishiwi; to the north the dark virgin timber of the Quetico; behind me—thirty hurtling, noise-packed minutes away—the pavements of the town I had left. The entire country seemed in flood, the network of waterways running into one another, filling all the valleys with their blue and white, every sunken spot between the hills.

I glanced at the map and saw that just ahead was Gabemichigami, a tremendous gash between two steep ridges. The plane banked, circled, and then, like the hawk it was, dropped to its kill, spiraling downward until it swooped close over the reaching tops of the pines. It side-slipped between the towering shores, and in a moment the pontoons were slapping the water as the plane nosed gently toward the shore.

The pilot threw out my pack, and I scrambled along the pontoon and jumped for the rocks. A farewell push and the wings turned toward the open lake once more. The engine roared and the plane moved out in a cloud of spray. A moment later it was in the air over the ridges, heading back toward town. I glanced at my watch. It was exactly thirty minutes since we took off and here I was alone, as I had planned it, deep in the heart of the wilderness at a point that normally would have taken several days of hard travel by canoe.

After the quiet had come again, I looked around me and found my old campsite as I had left it a year before. The balsam boughs were dried and withered over my bed and the pothooks were still in place over the fire. There was the same little creek tumbling down from the rocks in its escape from Little Saganaga to the east, the same swirling pool with its trout. I had dreamed of this spot, of being alone here for just one day, of taking one of the beautiful trout below the riffle and enjoying the old wilderness I had known. To my amazement, the dream had come true.

At first I could not realize the change, so violent had it been. Formerly, by the time I had reached this spot on the map, the country had had a chance to soak in and become a part of me. But as I stood listening to the far drone of the plane, I knew that I was still part of the environment I had left and that it would take time for the old feeling of wilderness to come.

I have known that feeling many times since. To leave New York in the evening and be in Los Angeles in the morning, or

Miami or Havana or Chicago in just a few hours, is a psychological shock. One is never prepared for the change of scene, and I sometimes wonder if one ever will be.

I strolled back over the portage to the dead water above the rapids and sat there a long time trying to recapture the feeling of accomplishment I had known the last time I came in, but all that came to me was the violent throbbing reaction to my flight and a jumble made up of the many things I had done in the last hour of preparation. When the tent was up and fresh boughs were cut for my bed, I busied myself with my rod and began to cast for a trout. Before long I had a fine three-pounder, one of the golden-brown lake trout that grow to their best in Gabemichigami. I caught three, all told, and for an hour had the excitement of good fishing.

But that night in front of the fire, listening to the loons and their echoing calls from Little Saganaga, Kekekabic, Ogish-gemuncie, and a hundred other lakes around, I knew the answer. This was what I had dreamed of doing, but for the first time in my life I had failed to work for the joy of knowing the wilderness; had not given it a chance to become a part of me. The last time it had taken three days of travel, many portages, sixty miles or more of bending to the paddle and fighting the wind, two campsites along the way, with always the great goal ahead, one of the most beautiful spots in the border country.

That vision alone had been enough to make my packs light and to take the sting from tired muscles. The thought of that camp with the creek singing away beside it was compensation enough. When at last after those days of travel my tent was actually pitched there, I knew real joy and happiness. This time it seemed that I had not earned the right to enjoy it.

The next afternoon the plane roared again over the horizon and in half an hour I was back to the automobiles, the pavements, and my friends. Yes, I had been on a flight, had gone far into the lake country, had taken a few trout and enjoyed myself, but inside I was still a little out of breath and somewhat baffled by what I had done. Seeing the country from the air had given me a bird's-eye view and perspective that I could not have in any other way, and the beauty was not lost to me.

I knew, however, what I must do the next time. I must go in with pack and canoe and work for the peace of mind which I knew could be found there. I would be a mole again and learn the feel of rocks under my feet, breathe the scent of balsam and spruce under the sun, feel the wetness of spray and muskeg, be part of the wilderness itself.

CHAPTER 7

FOREST POOL

A RING of spongy muskeg hemmed the pool, muskeg cut deep with game trails radiating from the water like the spokes of a wheel. Back of the muskeg was a rim of pointed spruce and beyond that a great wall of towering pines. The pool was the shining hub of the wheel, its black surface reflecting the protecting timber. The air was heavy with the redolence of sphagnum and resin. No sounds but those of the wilderness had ever penetrated there. At the close of its long primeval period, the pool lay perfect and untouched.

A hundred years ago a white trapper from the settlements to the south followed one of the game trails that lead to the pool. Trees were felled and he built a rough log shelter on the rise close to the edge of the muskeg, but even that did not change the quiet that had always reigned there. The nasal twang of the nuthatches still came from the pines, chickadees sang, and red squirrels leaped through the sunlit tops high above.

In the pines were marten, and in a swale not far away, beaver and otter. For many winters the trapper took his toll, and then the moose and caribou that used to come to the pool drifted to the north. The trap lines grew longer and longer, and one winter the trapper did not return. The cabin fell into decay, chinking dropped from between the logs, and at last the roof fell in. Pine needles and moss covered it, and after a time it became a mound of duff beneath the trees. Once more moose and caribou came down the trails and the marten were back in the timber. The forest pool lay as before, smooth and dark in the shadows.

Then, one fall, timber-cruisers discovered the pool and the great stand of pines around it. They repaired the old cabin, re-chinked the logs, replaced the roof. For months they worked, blazing long, straight lines through the surrounding forest, laying out roadways and trails, cruising the timber. In the spring,

118

when the campaign of destruction was complete, they left the pool and followed the trapper's trail toward the south.

It was September when the logging crews moved in with men and horses, mountains of equipment and supplies. They tethered their teams in the big timber around the pool. For days the woods resounded to the crash of falling trees, the shouts of men at work. Never for a moment were the axes silent or the cross-cut saws. Log buildings rose where the trees had been, and for the first time the forest pool knew the glare of sunlight. Until the snows came, moose and caribou returned to their old watering-place and the hunters who supplied the long tables with food shot what they needed without stirring far from camp.

For two winters the loggers stayed, and then they moved on to new stands of timber in the north. For many years the pool lay stripped and ugly, and around it the slashings were barren of life. Only the rabbits remained and the coyotes that preyed upon them. At first the pool had as much water as before, but when the little streams and spring trickles disappeared, it began to shrink and the once-spongy muskeg around it became brittle and dry.

After a summer's drought came a violent storm. Lightning flashed and thunder rolled over the denuded hills. After the storm had passed, a tall dead snag crackled and blazed. When it crashed into a tangle of brush and tinder-dry pine tops, the slash exploded, and for weeks the entire countryside lay under a pall of smoke.

Mosses and lichens disappeared, and then came fireweed.

jack pine, aspen, and birch. The water shrank still more in the old pool. Cattails and sphagnum encroached upon its edges from the surrounding muskeg and soon covered most of the open water. What little remained was green with algal scum.

Long after the fire a settler drove his team over one of the old logging roads to the site of the big logging camp at the pool. In the wagon were an ax, a saw, a breaking-plow, and supplies. At the swamp hole he watered his horses and stood there remembering the pines as they looked when he had come in with the crew. One small building had escaped the fire. He moved into it and set to work clearing himself a farm. Day and night he labored, pulling stumps and burning the great piles of roots and brush and windfalls left from the logging and the fire. Gradually a small field was broken to the plow.

As time went on, the little field grew larger and larger, but always in its center was the unsightly swamp hole, which defied all attempts at drainage—an ugly scar in his open clearing, a jungle of blackened and twisted roots interlaced with briars and alder. Because the pool bred mosquitoes, he built a new cabin on a hillside at the far edge of the field.

One day while he was working there, one of the horses wandered back to the swamp hole to crop the sedge, which was greener there than anywhere else. The animal went too close to the edge of the water, broke through the layer of muskeg which had almost overgrown it, became hopelessly mired, sank deeper and deeper into the muck. When the settler came, the horse was dead.

That day he built a rail fence around the pool and rode the

other horse to town for a box of dynamite. He knew what he must do: blast the layer of hardpan that lay beneath so the water could drain away.

In the fall when the swamp hole was dry, he dug down through the black peat, tamped in a charge of explosive, and lit the fuse. With a roar the blast went off and the swamp hole seemed to lift; roots and earth and stones mushroomed high into the air to fall again into the hole from which they had come. After that it was quiet and the air was acrid with the smell of burnt powder. The settler picked up a caribou horn that was golden-brown and in places blackened with age, and nailed it above the door of his cabin across the clearing.

The following spring the shining blade of the breaking-plow cut into the bottom of the little marsh, tearing through what was left of the ancient rim of sphagnum and the game trails that could still be dimly seen, trails that had been followed since the retreat of the glaciers to the north. Now for the first time furrows ran straight across the field. That summer the clearing was planted to corn, and when the crop was grown, it was hard to tell where the forest pool had been except that the stalks were taller there and darker green.

One night when the moon was full the settler walked out to the center of his field and stood there listening to the rustling of his corn. Now the whole field belonged to him and there was no longer the smell of the swamp, no longer anything to remind him of the old wilderness. It was even hard to remember how it had looked when the logging crews moved in. That had been a different world. Now the air was rich with the

scent of sweet clover and ripening corn. From the hillside beyond shone the lights of home, and he heard the soft tinkle of
a cowbell in the pasture back of the barn.

But as he stood there a great horned owl hooted back in the
woods, and for a moment the ancient scene returned. Again
the pool was there with its rim of pointed spruce and the tall
pines. There was a hint of sphagnum and resin in the night air
and the pool was silvered under the moon. Then just as swiftly
the vision was gone. The corn rustled softly and the tinkling
bell in the pasture was very clear.

CHAPTER 8

THE STONE WALL

WHENEVER life doesn't seem to be fun any more, I have an infallible cure; I go out and work on my wall—dig rocks out of the turf and move them from where they have been resting for ten thousand years or more to some place of my own choosing. Somehow when I do this the world moves off magically to where it belongs and I take the helm, no matter what the situation at the moment happens to be. This moving of stones is almost like the laying on of hands, except that in this case the process is reversed, for when I touch them I seem to exchange my little worries for some of their stability and calm.

I like stones. To me they are not dead or inert but as alive as the crystals that compose them. While they may appear unchangeable, I know that within them is a dynamic cosmos, each one with a character of its own and an indelible record of some phase of the earth's history.

They make me remember places I have seen: cliffs covered with mosses and harebells, roaring canyons in the wilderness, talus slopes where the marmots live, glaciated ridges, pebbled beaches and rocky shores. I like the rough feel of them and their weight, and the way the lichens and mosses have with them.

Not a stone in my wall but has a story to tell, not a one but brings back to me in a flash a vision of some place I have known. That wall is a record of my travels and an album of all creation, each stone a separate page from the long story of the past.

One section happens to be built of glacial boulders: granite and schist, red jasper veined with white quartz, greenstone and black basalt, and some whose names I do not pretend to know. Rounded by the rivers, lake shores, and coasts of the Hudson Bay country, they were gripped by the glacial ice and brought a thousand miles to the south. When the ice front retreated, they were dropped as terminal moraine on the hilltop where I live.

That was thousands of years ago, when the country was cold and devoid of life. Those rounded boulders had known the bitter years, had seen the first lichens and mosses that came to cover the scars of glaciation, had watched the slow formation of humus, an inch each thousand years, had felt at last the gripping roots of the tall red pines. They had seen the passing of the woodland caribou and the Indian tribes, were here when the white men moved in a century ago.

Then for the first time the scattered stones were moved by man and placed in great piles so the plow could go between. That is where I found most of them, hidden by the yellow and gold of sumac, cherry, and birch. Now, after all those centuries of waiting, the water- and ice-worn specimens from the entire Canadian shield had come to rest.

The large ones I built into the base, the smaller ones went on top, and the ones I knew best where I could always see them. They are the special ones whose stories are most meaningful to me. The common ones, the ordinary granites and schists and basalts, have their stories too, perhaps as vivid, if I knew them, as the rest. I do know the country they came from —have seen the very cliffs and shores from which they were broken ages ago. Each one of them gives me a sense of being a part of the wilderness from which they came.

One of my prizes is a boulder of rough conglomerate which at one time was part of an ocean shore. The matrix is mud compacted into slate, but the pebbles it holds are round and smooth, and I know they have been rolled by the tides and storms of some arctic coast. That stone brings back to me pictures of all the seashores I have ever known, of sunlight shining on the beaches, of moonlight on the surf and the roar of it at a time when no one was there to hear.

Another is a section of hard hematite ore veined with jasper and quartz. That stone is beautiful, banded in pink and dark red and metallic blue, with a lacework of snowy crystalline white. It goes back much further than the conglomerate, for the iron composing it was laid down by iron and sulphur bacteria, the first forms of life on this earth, organisms that had the faculty of building into their own microscopic structures raw iron from the earth's crust. When they died, great beds of iron-impregnated silt were deposited. Then after æons of volcanic action, leaching, gigantic pressures with molten lavas coursing through them, they formed at last the hematites that today produce the finest steel in the world.

Even though that bit of iron ore was old, I found a broken ledge of greenstone far more ancient than any other stone in the wall or, just possibly, in any wall on the face of the planet. That greenstone is part of the original crust formed when the molten lavas and gases first cooled. It came from the formation that underlies all others, has a tradition and permanence far more impressive than the glacial newcomers. I gave it a position suitable to its rank.

Another stone from a ledge of basalt is marked with glacial striæ cut when the ice sheet wore down the peaks of the old Vermilion Range. I found it one day while watching a gang of workmen excavating for a road. They had shoveled off the sand and gravel from the ledge preparatory to blasting, and for the first time since the retreat of the Laurentian Lobe of the glacier that surface was exposed to the light. I saw it then as all rock surfaces must have looked before the weather dulled their brilliance. That day it was as freshly polished as when newly scoured by the ice, and the scratches of gravel from the glacier's grinding base were as sharply defined as though they were newly gouged. The blast came and the ledge was scattered wide. I saved one perfect piece, and now it rests where I can always see it and remember its story.

One day I found a flat section of slate covered with ripple marks. The instant I saw it, I knew it must have a very special place, for that stone was at one time mud washed by the waters of some ancient sea. When the bottom was exposed to the sun or volcanic heat, those ripples of a bygone age were baked into shape for all time. Those gray-green rippled surfaces had captured the movement of an ocean, its aliveness and constant change. After a rain the slate glistens and shines and the ripple marks look fresh. It rests proudly on top of the wall, a part of the ocean floor.

When I built a fireplace in one corner of the wall, I knew that it must be faithful to the Canadian shield; whatever went into it must somehow tell the story of the entire lake country of the north. And so I built into it samples of all the native types from hundreds of miles around, sections from the ridges, rivers, and lake shores which would bring memories of all the country that voyageurs had traveled and explored. I whittled a set of wooden pothooks and a tea stick, and built a fire to darken the stones so that any canoeman coming by would catch his breath in recognition.

That cruiser's fireplace is a bit of the wilderness, a symbol of the companionship I have known on many expeditions into the north. When I kindle a fire there and see those rough, familiar rocks reflecting its glow, friends of the trail stand beside me and talk to me out of the past.

CHAPTER 9

SILENCE

I T WAS before dawn, that period of hush before the birds had begun to sing. The lake was breathing softly as in sleep; rising and falling, it seemed to me to absorb like a great sponge all the sounds of the earth. It was a time of quiet—no wind rustling the leaves, no lapping of the water, no calling of animals or birds. But I listened just the same, straining with all my faculties toward something—I knew not what—trying to catch the meanings that were there in that moment before the lifting of the dark.

Standing there alone, I felt alive, more aware and receptive than ever before. A shout or a movement would have destroyed the spell. This was a time for silence, for being in pace with ancient rhythms and timelessness, the breathing of the lake, the slow growth of living things. Here the cosmos could be felt and the true meaning of attunement.

I once climbed a great ridge called Robinson Peak to watch the sunset and to get a view of the lakes and rivers below, the rugged hills and valleys of the Quetico-Superior. When I reached the bald knob of the peak the sun was just above the horizon, a flaming ball ready to drop into the dusk below. Far beneath me on a point of pines reaching into the lake was the white inverted V of my tent. It looked very tiny down there where it was almost night.

As I watched and listened, I became conscious of the slow, steady hum of millions of insects and through it the calling of the whitethroats and the violin notes of the hermit thrushes. But it all seemed very vague from that height and very far away, and gradually they merged one with another, blending in a great enveloping softness of sound no louder, it seemed, than my breathing.

The sun was trembling now on the edge of the ridge. It was alive, almost fluid and pulsating, and as I watched it sink I thought that I could feel the earth turning from it, actually feel its rotation. Over all was the silence of the wilderness, that sense of oneness which comes only when there are no distracting sights or sounds, when we listen with inward ears and see with inward eyes, when we feel and are aware with our entire beings rather than our senses. I thought as I sat there of the ancient admonition "Be still and know that I am God," and knew that without stillness there can be no knowing, without divorcement from outside influences man cannot know what spirit means.

One winter night I stood and listened beneath the stars. It was cold, perhaps twenty below, and I was on a lake deep in the wilds. The stars were close that night, so close they almost blazed, and the Milky Way was a brilliant luminous splash across the heavens. An owl hooted somberly in the timber of the dark shores, a sound that accentuated the quiet on the open lake. Here again was the silence, and I thought how rare it is to know it, how increasingly difficult to ever achieve real quiet and the peace that comes with it, how true the statement "Tranquillity is beyond price."

More and more do we realize that quiet is important to our happiness. In our cities the constant beat of strange and foreign wave lengths on our primal senses beats us into neuroticism, changes us from creatures who once knew the silences to fretful, uncertain beings immersed in a cacophony of noise which destroys sanity and equilibrium.

In recognition of this need, city churches leave their doors open so that people may come off the streets and in the semi-darkness find the quiet they need. I know a great sanctuary whose doors open onto one of the busiest and noisiest streets of the world. I go in there whenever I pass, and as the doors close behind me and I look up to the stained-glass windows and in the dusk sometimes hear the muted chords of a great organ, the quiet returns and I sense the silence once more. Beneath that vaulted dome is a small part of the eternal quiet the outside world once knew.

In Winchester Cathedral in England is a stained-glass window dedicated to Izaak Walton, the patron saint of all anglers. In the base of that window are four words that embody the philosophy of all who enjoy the gentle art of fishing and the out-of-doors:

STUDY TO BE QUIET

It is the key to all he ever wrote and thought about. Beside the rivers Itchen and Dove, Izaak Walton fished for peace and quiet, sought the silences and the places where thoughts were long and undisturbed.

Silence belongs to the primitive scene. Without it the vision of unchanged landscape means little more than rocks and trees and mountains. But with silence it has significance and meaning. What would the Grand Canyon's blue immensities and enormous depths, its sense of timelessness, be like with a helicopter roaring the length of it?

John Muir said: "The sequoias belong to the solitudes and the millenniums." Those ancient trees, some of them old before the birth of Christ, mature long before the continent was discovered, have among them the stillness of the ages. As such, they are more than trees; their very existence is sobering to short-lived man.

What would the wilderness lake country of the Quetico-Superior be like with the roar of airplane motors and high-powered transportation engulfing it? The charm of a canoe trip is in the quiet as one drifts along the shores, being a part of rocks and trees and every living thing. How swiftly it changes if all natural sounds are replaced by the explosive violence of combustion engines and speed. At times on quiet waters one does not speak aloud but only in whispers, for then all noise is sacrilege.

How much more one enjoys a countryside when walking through it! The sounds of the road, the constant sense of the mechanical detract from the complete enjoyment that means recreation and reversal of the type of experience we are accustomed to in everyday life. So often holidays are merely an extension of the identical influences we seek to escape. The fact that we have changed the scene makes little difference unless there is the compensating fact of quiet.

One does not have to be alone to enjoy silence. It has often been said that the ability to enjoy it with others is the mark of friendship and understanding. Only when people are strangers do they feel obliged to be entertaining. Where there is agreement and appreciation, silence is no bar to mutual enjoyment. When I have been alone in quiet places, I have often wished someone could share it and make the experience even richer and more complete.

PART TWO: SUMMER

How often we speak of the great silences of the wilderness and of the importance of preserving them and the wonder and peace to be found there! When I think of them, I see the lakes and rivers of the north, the muskegs and the expanses of tundra, the barren lands beyond all roads. I see the mountain ranges of the west and the high, rolling ridges of the Appalachians. I picture the deserts of the southwest and their brilliant panoramas of color, the impenetrable swamplands of the south. They will always be there and their beauty may not change, but should their silences be broken, they will never be the same.

AUTUMN

CHAPTER I

SCRUB OAK

WE BROUGHT the maples into
the yard so that we could enjoy for a few short days in the fall
the brilliant reds and yellows of their coloring, so they could
remind us of the flaming pageantry of the entire north whenever we looked their way, the poetry of shorelines and protected bays, the magic of seeing a lone and vivid splash of red

139

against a whole hillside of somber green. We wanted them to remind us of the portages of October and old logging roads carpeted with their fallen leaves. The maples are through swiftly, and when their sudden ecstasy is over, they stand bare and gray with nothing to soften the rigidity of their branches. But in the spring they are again the first, with bursting crimson buds as brilliant as those of any flowers in the north.

We brought the aspen in for many special reasons all their own. They are warm and friendly trees, and in the whispering of their leaves all summer long is a sense of gentleness. Although they are not long-lived, they will grow almost anywhere in open sunlight. The wood is soft, having neither the hardness of the maple nor the strength of pine, but back in the bush country the beaver depend upon it for food and canoemen for the finest firewood in the lake regions. Beaverwood, dry for many years on top of some old abandoned house— what better smokeless flame can a man want for his reflector oven, what greater cheer than its bright and eager burning? But it is in the fall when the aspen's leaves are masses of old gold and the hillsides and islands are mirrored in a sea of blue that the days become enchanted and a hush lies like a benediction over the entire country. Our clump of aspen would bring us all that.

We brought in the white birch because we wanted a reminder of immaculate stands of them straight and white against the brown of hillsides. We wanted to remember how they looked in midwinter when under the light of the moon they changed to misty silver, ephemeral against the snow. We wanted to watch them in the spring when the massed brown of winter slowly changed to the warmth of purple and mauve as the sap began to flow. They would remind us, too, of the part they played in the drama of discovery and exploration, for without great stands of birch there would have been no bark canoes, no voyageurs and their brigades from Montreal and Quebec, no Grand Portage, no fur trade in the far northwest. Most of all, they would remind us of places we loved— of Hula Lake perhaps on a sunny day in October when the rice beds of the Chippewas lay like a golden carpet over the blue of the water and the birches at the end of the portage stood white and gold against the sky.

And now we wanted one more tree, a tree different from all the rest, with a personality and character of its own. It would not be a tree that gave much color to the country in the fall, or one that was startlingly beautiful in the spring. Those qualities we already had in the maple, the birch, and the aspen. What we wanted now was a little scrub oak, one that combined certain qualities that none of the others had, an oak that held its leaves, that had grown where survival was tough and at the end of the year flaunted a bit of color when all the rest of the trees were drab. It could not be just an ordinary scrub oak, but the best of its kind, for what we wanted to bring into the yard this time was far more than just another tree.

Leaving home one morning in late October, we paddled through several lakes toward a high, rocky ridge where we knew they grew. A storm had stripped the color from shorelines and islands, and where a short time before the maples had flamed and the hills had been golden, there was now no remnant of the glory they had known. As we drifted toward the ridge we searched the shores for a last cluster of leaves which might have withstood the storm, some little oak tougher and more resistant than all the rest.

In the shallows were the remains of the color, the yellows and golds and reds, moving slowly, shifting position with the movement of the water, covering the bottom with an ever changing kaleidoscope of pattern and light. And then far up on the ridge we found what we were looking for, a lone spot of dark red, a final gesture of defiance to the storm, the only bit of brightness in that whole blended fusion of grays and browns and greens. We beached the canoe and began to climb, discovering that the way was hard—sheer cliffs, tangled gullies grown with hazel, windfalls one on top of another all the long climb up. At last we emerged on a smooth, barren ridge, and there was a small clump of scrub oak, its leaves still intact, their dark and shining mahogany a triumphant banner over the deserted battlefield. Whipped by many storms, the little clump had been beaten into a shape that seemed to embrace the glaciated knob of granite on which it grew. This was what we wanted. Here were character and strength.

The clump was growing from a crevice in the rock, its roots penetrating deep into the ledge itself, exploring hidden pockets of humus and moisture, twining themselves so tightly into the bed rock that no winds could ever pull them free. No other trees were there, no maple, aspen, or birch. They needed far more than the ridge could offer. That hard little hilltop belonged to the oak alone.

We sat beside the clump and studied it. It had a toughness and a certain wirelike hardness that all the others lacked. The species actually seemed to thrive upon adversity and to seek out places where survival was a struggle, the rocky, sandy, wind-swept environments where the elements combined to dwarf and limit all other growth by making life almost impossible. We had watched them in the spring and all through the seasons. Only after the more frivolous species had gone into the first wild abandon of bursting buds and flowers did the oaks bestir themselves. Even then they leaved out cautiously, as though not quite trusting the first warm zephyrs from the south. Then during the short summer months, while the rest of the trees and shrubs were luxuriating in an abundance of fertility, they fought for existence so that the leaves they finally brought forth might get their rightful inheritance before the cold winds of autumn fell upon them.

The aspen, the birch, and the maples colored almost overnight, but the oaks, conservative to the end, slowly turned to deep and shining red and finally to a waxy, gleaming mahogany. But when the storms came out of the north and the brilliant ones stood stripped and bare, they were fully clothed and far more beautiful than the rest had ever been because they stood alone.

The clump itself was far too large to move and the roots too deeply entwined in the crevices of the rock. Walking around it, I looked for a stray shoot that might have grown from a root or sprouted from a buried acorn. I found exactly what I wanted, a tiny dwarf of a tree growing well away from the main clump. I examined it closely, for I did not want to make a mistake and touch it unless I was sure it had a chance of survival. Not more than eighteen inches high and a quarter of an inch in diameter at the base of the stem, it was well shaped and had three full-sized mahogany leaves at its tip. I felt around its base and found that the roots were completely grown into a single fissure filled with the long accumulation of humus from mosses and lichens. While a few of the finer roots had gone deeper, the bulk of them were tightly entwined around the soil of the crevice.

With my knife I sliced carefully around its edges, loosened the tight net of roots from its holdfasts to the rock surfaces, then lifted out the complete mesh without losing or destroying any part of it. Wrapping the tiny bundle of roots and humus in a bandanna, we started down the ridge toward the canoe, realizing that we had a prize, that in our hands was the spirit of all the scrub oaks of the north.

We planted the oak in a corner of the stone wall close to the boulders so it would feel at home and have some protection while it was resetting its roots in the glacial gravel of the ridge on which we live. When the soil was packed around it, we watered it and covered the bruised earth with leaves and grass so it would look as though nothing had been disturbed.

When finished, we surveyed our work. A single leaf remained as a reminder of the hilltop where we had found the tree, one tiny fleck of color by the wall. No winter winds would ever break this tree's branches. They might bend and twist with the sleet and snow, but they would never break. It would stand there as a symbol of the indomitable, proof that a tree can learn to live with adversity. This oak would be an antidote for softness in our environment, a contrast to the summer lushness of other trees, of grass and flowers. While they had their brief sway of glory, it would be building up its strength, and only when they were forgotten would it come into its own.

It would grow slowly, consolidate its new position, and be there in its corner long after we were gone and perhaps long after the other trees had died. In time it would be as large perhaps as the mother clump from which it had sprung. It would always stand there before the coming of the snows, holding on to its final bit of color, and those who knew its story would remember the barren ridge from which it had come and the reason for its planting.

CHAPTER 2

WILD GEESE

Iᴛ ᴡᴀs November and I was
on top of a high, birch-covered ridge. The air was rich with
the smell of down leaves and the ground was covered with
bronze and tarnished gold. Far below was a blue lake with a
rice-filled river flowing into it. Where the river met the open
water, the rice fanned out like a golden apron, solidly colored

146

at the gathered waist, flecked with blue toward its fringes.

Suddenly out of the north came the sound I had been waiting for, a soft, melodious gabbling that swelled and died and
increased in volume until all other sounds were engulfed by
its clamor. Far in the blue I saw them, a long skein of dots undulating like a floating ribbon pulled toward the south by an
invisible cord tied to the point of its V.

I have never killed a goose and now I never intend to; the
sight and the sound of them is enough. But there was a time
when, more than anything else in the world, I wanted to bring
one of those high wanderers down to earth. The sound of wild
geese on the move haunted me and I felt that somehow I must
capture some of their mystery, some of their freedom and of
the blue distances into which they disappeared. The idea grew
into an obsession, and I used to lie awake at night, dreaming
and planning how I would bring it about. I never went hunting without a handful of shells loaded with buckshot, never
heard the grand music without praying that the birds would
come close. I do not believe that there was ever a boy who
wanted a goose as badly as I did. It was not just a case of being
able to say: "I killed a goose," though in my country, well out
of the main flyways, that would have been something to boast
about. It was far more than that; it was involved with the way
I felt and with the wonder of listening to them as they came
year after year and wove their way into space.

There was a time when a flock of them alighted in an open
field and I crawled on my belly for a mile, praying every foot
of the way that the birds would not see the waving of the

stubble, that they would keep on feeding until I was within range. That day there were other flocks in the air and the wind was alive with their calling. I can still hear those geese gabbling softly to themselves as they fed on the down grain, still see the long necks, the outstretched heads of the sentinels as I drew near. Then just when I was at the limit of range, a crow flew over, cawing its find to the world. They took to the air with a thunder of wings and I lay there a bare hundred yards away, watching them disappear over the horizon.

Another time, when the sun was setting over the marshes of Totogatik Lake, the wild gabbling came out of the north and the birds were silhouetted against a flaming sky. That time they caught me in the open between the rice and the tall grass near shore, but it was dusk and the canoe blended into its background. That instant is burned into my memory: the water like wine, the approaching flock, black spruce etched against the sky. Then they came, down—down—down out of the gloom until I could feel the measured beat of their wings. As they swung to land, a hunter fired from the far shore. They swerved and went out the way they had come.

A third time, in the hills during deer season, I heard a flock circling and circling, looking for a spot of open water. I knew a man who had shot one with a rifle; I had talked to him and wondered enviously if I would ever have such luck. The birds were big, their flight slow, and if you held right, your chances were good; but when the flock finally swung over that day in the hills, though they were well within range, nothing happened. Only a lone wing feather floated down, spiraling lazily out of the cold November sky.

Then one year my great chance came. I had been following a trail through a black spruce swamp on my way to the river, where I hoped to find a few last mallards feeding in the rice. It was in the very center of the bog that I heard them—just the merest hint of melody, but enough to stop me in my tracks. The flock was far away and almost instantly the sound was gone. Mallards were forgotten, everything else in the world but the geese circling the bend in the river. I reloaded my gun with buckshot, checked and rechecked my safety, placed the duck loads where I could not possibly make a mistake. Nothing must go wrong now. This was the time I had been praying for.

I stood there straining to catch the music again, but the moss-hung spruces and the soft cushion of muskeg seemed to absorb it. Suddenly the sound grew louder, changed in a moment from a vague, blended harmony to the clear, joyous clamor of birds coming in to feed. As yet I could see nothing, but the music rose and fell as the flock dipped between the hills and valleys looking for a place to land. Then they were overhead and their bugling filled the trees, and I ran madly for the closest ridge where I might have a chance of seeing them as they came by. I plunged through the tangle of heather and sphagnum beneath the spruces, scrambled up the rocks to the crest of the ridge. They had seen the patch of rice in the river, had spotted the blue open water, and would have to circle close to the ledge in order to land. Wild, impossible thoughts were mine that day, but nothing was impossible then.

I was breathless when I reached the top. From where I stood, I commanded a clear view of the swamp, the winding blue of the river, the golden spot of rice in the mallard hole. The din of their calling grew louder and at last was so deafening that the rocks themselves seemed to bounce back the sound. Then they were directly above and I could see the outstretched necks with their white chin straps, the snowy undersides of the wings.

Straight overhead now in a wavering V, still just out of range. I crouched against a boulder and prayed that they would swing back. For a moment they disappeared behind a ridge, and as the calling died I was sick at heart, knowing I should have taken my chance and fired.

Then they were back, and as they sailed over the spruce tops I knew this was the moment I had been waiting for. They were much bigger than I had ever imagined. I could not only hear the beat of their wings and the rush of air through them, but could actually feel it. At that moment they seemed almost close enough to touch and I could see their eyes, the wary turning of their heads, their outstretched feet. Then they saw me there against the rock and pandemonium broke loose. The flock climbed into the sky, beat the air desperately to escape. Not until then did I remember my gun and what I had come for, and now it was too late. The birds were out of range.

After that boyhood experience I never tried to kill a goose, and now that I am older and a little wiser, I think I know the reason why. As I look back, I could comfort the boy I was. I could tell him that one should never try to capture something as wild and beautiful as the calling of geese, that it is better to wait and listen as they go by and wonder where they have gone. But, knowing that boy, I realize that he would not believe me. Only many years could heal the wound of that October day.

The long skein of dots was fading into the horizon and the calling grew fainter and fainter. Then for a moment it was gone and I heard it almost as a remembered sound. Once more it came and I caught the lift of the flock just before it was swallowed in the blue. There was the lake far below me and the rice-filled golden river running into it, and the air was rich with the smell of down leaves.

CHAPTER 3

THE RED SQUIRREL

THE canoe was getting heavy, its carrying-yoke biting into my shoulders, the pack straps cutting my wind. I had come this way to see the big timber along the portage and to get the feel of the duff once more before the coming of the snow. This would be one of the last portages of the season and I wanted to remember it as something special, but as I staggered on beneath my load, I realized that æsthetic enjoyment and packing are not always complementary; that there is not the full appreciation of smells and vistas and sounds when every step is an effort.

There was a steep rise ahead. I dug in my toes, carried the canoe almost straight upward, somehow found the breath and energy to reach the top. There in a patch of pines I dropped my load and sank down wearily beside it.

It was good to rest, good to breathe evenly once more, to see out of eyes no longer bleared with sweat. Nothing could ever be more completely satisfying than rest after a long portage. Gradually my heart stopped its pounding and my breathing became quiet. I stretched out on a smooth carpet of needles and looked up through the pines to the blue sky overhead. It was late October and the woods were hushed. A hairy woodpecker began its hammering on a dead stub, so loud that it sounded like a pneumatic drill. When it stopped, the hush was deeper than ever.

Even the scurrying of a red-backed mouse through the leaves startled me, and then as I lay there I became conscious of a steady rustling coming from everywhere at once. It wasn't loud, and at first I was not aware of it at all, but gradually as I became quiet the steady rustling became distinct, a dry moving in the leaves and in the tops of the pines. The squirrels were at their work, reaping a harvest of cones before the first November gale.

From out of a tangle of brush beside the trail emerged a plump, well-colored oldster, a veritable alderman of a squirrel.

For a moment he eyed me merrily and then, within three feet of my boot, buried a cone. When he had finished, he sat on his haunches, appraised me thoughtfully, and then, as though satisfied that I was of no great importance in his scheme of things, scrambled into a spruce near by. There, after a hurried selection, he cut another cone and proceeded to peel it right above me, the tiny bracts showering all around. Presently he flipped the core and tore down the scaly trunk in a flurry of bark.

I have always liked squirrels with their eternal busyness and chatter. Of all the animals in the woods, I believe they have given me the most pleasure. What would a campsite be like without a squirrel or two to watch? I like the warm heather brown of their coloring, the rim of white around the eyes, the creamy contrast of the underside. And those beautiful tails: is there any animal that can match them either in appearance or as a means of expression? Squirrels have always interested me, and ever since I was old enough to explore the woods on my own, I have tried to know them.

No matter where you go, you find them. On this portage in the north they were no different, barring coloring and size, from those I had known in the cypress swamps of the south, the mountains of the west, or the oak-hickory forests of the east. Always they were there, the same curious, friendly little creatures I had known at home.

In spite of my lifelong interest in the species, I must confess that I have neglected utterly all scientific aspects, and without a doubt zoologists will rank me as a disgrace to the profession. I do know that the chap who just sailed across the pine tops is known by the awe-inspiring name of *Sciurus hudsonicus* (Erxleben), and that ecologically he is considered a secondary influent of the biome, which means in simple language that he plants pine trees by forgetting where he stores his cones in the soil beneath the duff. In fact, foresters agree that without him there would be very little natural reproduction in old timber stands.

I also know that owls like them as well as martens, and that they can throw the fear of death into the larger gray squirrels, should they invade, through the convenient medium of castration. Outside of such vital facts, I have carried on no research, have gathered no pertinent data, nothing that might give the species the rightful position it deserves in the ecological community. I have never bothered to count or describe their dentition, have never measured their gorgeous tails with a millimeter rule, have no long rows of neatly stuffed skins properly labeled with dates, habitats, and the names of species and subspecies. The relationship of such vital factors as temperature and humidity to the phenomenon of hibernation has interested me not at all. Gestation periods, stomach analysis, and population cycles are closed books to me. Not once have I been tempted to contribute an article on them to the scientific journals, for what I have learned about squirrels and their ways is of no importance to anyone but myself.

My interest in squirrels has been purely one of friendship and appreciation. To me they are symbolic of the wilderness places I have known all over the continent. They are as wonderful to me as any of the larger forms of mammals, as indicative of the old America as the trees themselves. What better way of thinking of the ancient forests of the continent than to realize that a squirrel could have run through the tops of them from the Atlantic coast to the Mississippi without having to come to earth?

My acquaintanceship with squirrels has been a long one: even as a boy I haunted the places where they lived. I became so expert in squirrel lore that I could tell by merely walking through a woods if they were there. A swift glance at a runway log and I knew if it was being used. They were so much a part of my boyhood that I know they must have flashed across my dreams.

There was a time when I wanted more than anything else in the world to catch a squirrel and have it for my own. I felt then as I did about many things: that if I could actually achieve personal possession, my enjoyment would somehow be complete. I wanted to feed one of the little creatures, care for it, and lavish my affection upon it. The idea that I would be depriving it of freedom never entered my thinking.

As I rested on the portage that day, the years rolled swiftly away and I was in another old stand of pine timber trying to catch my first squirrel. My box trap, baited with a clump of hazel nuts, was set on a moss-covered log, a runway from one pine to another.

That day a squirrel came spiraling down the trunk of a pine, chattering and scolding every foot of the way. I froze into the stump behind me. Just above me it stopped, eyed me for a moment, and then, with a free and reckless leap, landed on the very end of the log on which the trap was set. Down the wide green trail it came. It had seen the bait, was at the door, and with a scurry of tail was inside. Then with a crash the door came down and the squirrel was mine. The miracle had happened and I had taken something wild and beautiful as my own. The moment was burned into my memory.

Back home, I spent hours watching it, fed it only the choicest of nuts and cones, replenished each day the branches of pine and hemlock within the cage. At last it came to know me and took tidbits from my fingers, and I came to know the squirrel, its mannerisms, its habits of feeding and drinking, resting and playing. Later on I caught its mate the same way, and when the female lined the nest with fur from its own breast my happiness was complete.

Then one morning the little family was gone, a neatly gnawed hole my only clue. For days I searched the trees around my home, haunted the woodpiles and the logs, but never again did I see them. That had been long ago, and now as I sat against my canoe, watching the squirrels scurrying up and down the trees and scolding me from the branches above, I knew that my particular investigation had stood the test of time; that, while I had contributed nothing of scientific value regarding the species, squirrels had contributed a great deal to me in ways that could not be recorded.

A pair dashed across the trail, scrambled fiercely up the scaly trunk of a red pine, chased each other out to the very tip of a high, swinging branch, and then with reckless abandon hurled themselves through space.

PART THREE: AUTUMN

It was getting late and I had a long way to go before dark. In the lake country, canoes are made to portage and paddle, not to rest against. As I rose to my feet the scurrying stopped and the quiet of the October day descended once more. A last look around, a deep breath, and I swung the canoe onto my shoulders, settled it, and moved on toward the end of the portage and the last lake of my route.

CHAPTER 4

CARIBOU MOSS

I HAVE climbed to the very top of a high granite ridge. There from a bare glaciated dome I look down over the blue, sparkling sweep of Shagawa Lake with its clustered rocky islands. On the south shore of the lake is the little mining town of Ely with its closely packed houses, its spiderlike shafts and trestles, its stock piles of reddish iron ore. Below is Lamb's Creek, winding with many twists and turns through an old beaver meadow. To the north and west are tumbled ridges and valleys, and over all is a sense of freedom and expansiveness.

There are many reasons for climbing this ridge at any season of the year. In the spring when the stand of slender aspen just below is brushed with light green and the hermit thrushes are in full song, the valley is a symphony. I like it in the summer when nighthawks zoom in wide, circling sweeps above it, and in the fall when an orange hunter's moon floods the wilderness with its light. Even in the dead of winter the climb is worth while just to see the sculptured drifts and the smooth white surfaces of snow.

Here the caribou moss grows and has never been disturbed. Where I rest, the rosy matrix of granite is crisscrossed with veins of snowy quartz. Huge crystals of feldspar, hornblend, and mica lace the borders of those veins, evidence of slowness of cooling when the granite was spewed from some volcanic throat. In those veins and in thousands of tiny fissures grow tufts of the silvery-gray moss. A glacial groove leads from one end of the dome to the other. Gouged ten thousand years ago by a hard rock in the base of the ice, it provided a growing-place for the first spores that drifted across the ridge after the recession. There the caribou moss is growing and will continue to grow for centuries to come.

Those silvery little tufts before me are the shock troops of the north, the commandos with which the plant kingdom made a beachhead on a barren, rocky ridge. Surviving where other types would die, needing nothing but crystalline rocks and air, they prepare the way for occupation and for the communities to come.

Caribou moss is a lichen and therefore a pioneer among plants, taking root on any barren, rocky surface where broken crystalline structure will hold the spores. Any surface rough enough to catch one can be the starting-point of growth. In such places the rootlike hyphæ with their acid exudate dissolve the mineral substance of granite, greenstone, and basalt, widening and deepening the fissures. Water seeps into them and frost breaks them further still, and in time they are covered with lichens. Humus forms beneath them and gradually washes into the deeper cracks until the stage is set for seeds of herbs and shrubs and even trees.

All around me is evidence of the slow invasion of forest types. While the granite surfaces of the rock mass are still covered with lichens, along its edges gnarled and stunted pines, junipers, and cedars are reaching down into the rock itself, forcing huge slabs away from the ridge, breaking and probing new pathways for their ever hungry roots. Eventually those hardy little trees will take over the dome itself. Thousands of years may be needed to pave the way, with countless defeats for the tiny seedlings, but in time, in spite of storm and flood and bitter cold, they will win, and the lichens that have made it possible will be relegated to the remaining fringes beyond the rooted trees.

Some lichens are like cracked and brittle paint against the rock, others like old-fashioned gray-green rosettes, but the caribou moss is like dwarf clumps of leafless shrubs. Strange and wonderful, it is actually a combination of two different plants—one whose rootlets can break down the rock, the other embedded deep within its tissues, a green and globular alga. The algæ possess green chloroplasts which through the alchemy of water, air, and sunlight provide the host with the starch it cannot produce itself. The host in turn provides the moisture and the elements of growth from the mineral rock it has dissolved. Partners in one of the first co-operative ventures in the plant kingdom, one plant cannot get along without the other. How such an arrangement came about is one of the marvels of evolutionary progression. Happenstance? A conceived master plan? Science can only guess and may never know.

This we do know: the matrix of the master plan is as infinite as the universe itself, and its minutest dependencies are as profound as its greater counterparts.

Near by is a deep cushion of caribou moss. It is damp with dew, soft and resilient as spun rubber. It shines with a luster that is now grayish-green, now the color of old and tarnished silver. Down the center of the bed is a reddish scar, a thin line of blueberry plants already turned by the frost. Underneath that crimson line is a crack in the bed rock filled with the accumulated humus of centuries of growth. Someday a squirrel will bury a cone there; if the seeds germinate, the roots of a tree may find the soil, and then, in time, the luxurious carpet of moss will be covered with duff.

This morning the caribou moss is alive and growing, but by noon the drying sun will stop all activity of the algæ within it. A prolonged dry spell and the delicate stems will be like powder, crunch like brittle glass underfoot. A rain, a fall of dew, and it will swiftly spring to life. Survival is no problem.

Cladonia rangiferine the botanists call it, the most common of all the lichens in the forested regions of the Quetico-Superior. A century ago the food of the woodland caribou, with the advent of logging, forest fires, and the coming in of aspen and birch it disappeared over great areas. The caribou drifted to regions beyond, to the solitudes of the barren lands still undisturbed by man. Now, with the spruce and pine and balsam again covering the valleys and ridges, the caribou moss is everywhere, and though the caribou have not returned, their ancient range is waiting.

In northern Europe and Iceland the lichens have served as food during periods of famine, and it is well known that in our own north they have kept many a wilderness traveler from starvation. French voyageurs called the large, leafy growths on the cliffs *tripe du roche*, or rock tripe, because of the close resemblance of its underside to the tripe obtained from the lining of a cow's stomach. When boiled, it makes a gelatinous meringue that, though not a gourmet's delight, will keep a man alive. In the deserts of Africa there is a legend that certain lichens may have saved the Israelite tribes from death during their long migration from Egypt to the promised land. Natives of the region still call it "Manna from Heaven."

Caribou moss tells me many things, imparts to me something of its own association with distances and solitude. Part of the ice-worn rocks of the Canadian Shield, at one with northern lights and waterways and the sub-arctic wilderness, it is symbolic not only of an environment but of a way of life as well.

CHAPTER 5

PINE KNOTS

PINE knots are different from ordinary firewoods. They cannot be compared with birch or aspen or oak, for the time-and-effort cost of gathering them is beyond the realm of common sense and reason. The warmth they give is negligible, but the light effects when they burn have a quality and importance that none of the others can approach. The burning of an old pine knot is a spiritual occasion, and the possession of a goodly supply for winter nights before the fireplace is a joy.

It was late October when I made my last expedition for knots. I say "expedition" because each foray after the prized nuggets of resin is more like a hunting-trip than ordinary wood-gathering. You just do not go into the woods anywhere, but must know the terrain and something about the ecology of the forests in order to know where to find them. More important than anything else is to be in the proper frame of mind, to recognize their worth, and to embark in a spirit of adventure.

Ice was forming in the protected bays of the lake the day I set forth. There was barely a quarter of an inch near shore, but enough to scratch the sides of the canoe. The leaves were gone and only in the hollows was there any remnant of the rusty bronze of the birches. Even the old gold of the tamaracks had disappeared and now they stood sere and gray in the bogs, waiting for the snow. The grasses were yellowed and in a little bay were covered with frost crystals. As the canoe slipped by, they moved suddenly in a breath of air and the bay sparkled with millions of sequins. A lone flock of bluebills took wing from the open water, circled warily, and disappeared over the horizon.

I landed the canoe on a grassy slope crowned with birches. Here at one time grew tall pines—not that there were any stumps or logs in evidence, but the mounds that marked their falling showed me where they had lain. Underneath the leaves and the duff were the knots, hard and sound and heavy. They would burn like torches, hold their flames as though unwilling to squander the energy they had held so long.

Near the landing I found several weathered to a silver gray, pointed spindles washed and polished by the waves until they were smooth and symmetrical. They had come from a pine that had dropped toward the water, and I could see its ancient top in the depths away from shore.

When I explored beneath the leaves, I found some sections of wood with the knots still in place. A blow of the ax and they were free for the taking. But mostly the knots lay by themselves with the brown disintegration of bark and wood still around them. I soon had a good pile of them down by the canoe.

Here was the same primitive satisfaction one finds fishing and hunting or in picking berries. The closest thing to it in wood-gathering is the stealing from abandoned beaver lodges of peeled and clean sticks of aspen that have served their purpose long ago. Like finding knots, it is living off the country, bringing in something from the wilds which no one else could find for you, something you would not want anyone else to do because of the joy of doing it yourself.

Knowing how the knots were made gives them significance, makes them unique and different from any other plant structure. All pines have resin ducts through which the golden fluid travels from the roots to the highest twigs. Where branches leave the main trunk, these ducts are bent, and because of the bending the flow of resin is dammed, saturating and completely impregnating the wood fibers. The same thing happens in gnarled and twisted roots, in any place where the free flow of resin is slowed. Although a great log may crumble into dust, the resin-soaked knots are impervious to decay and stay on for many years.

That night I stopped at the cabin of an old woodsman who felt about knots and resinous wood as I did. We had in common a vast respect for pine and what it could do. Before I crawled into my sleeping-bag, I watched him go through the ritual he had followed for many years. In back of his barrel stove were several sticks of red pine, sticks as dry and full of pitch as he could find. I watched him select a piece, turn it over carefully in his hands, then seat himself with his back against the wall.

Very deliberately he shaved off the first long shavings, each one curling beautifully as it left the blade. The longer and thinner the shaving, the better the curl; the tighter the curl, the quicker the flame. The knife sliced through again and again, and with each slice the contentment on the face of my friend seemed to grow. He contemplated the pile with satisfaction and watched the shavings twist and curl as though they were alive in the warmth of the barrel stove.

"Nothing better," he said. "Got a fine smell, too." He handed me a stick to smell. "That would explode when the flame hit it," he said.

The pile of feathered sticks and shavings was large enough. He pushed it carefully away from the stove to a spot against the wall where it would bask in the heat most of the night and in the morning be crisp and ready to flame. He sheathed his knife, for the ritual was over, the same ritual that in thousands of cabins and farm kitchens all over the land had been routine for generations. Here was real work, as important in its way as the setting of bread or the breaking of ground. This was purposeful, primitive, and satisfying, and most surely promoted pleasant dreams.

How much better, I thought, would it be for city nerves if at the close of each day a man could put his back to the wall and in the warmth of a barrel stove, with the wind and sleet whipping into a gale outside, whittle himself a pile of fragrant pine shavings. How much more serene his slumbers than if he simply checked his thermostat.

When I returned home the following day, I stored my knots in a special place where no one would make the mistake of taking them for ordinary wood. After hunting for them, packing them across the portages, and paddling them down several waterways, I would not let them be burned indiscriminately. They were reserved for special occasions when there was good talk, and music, and when the fire had burned to a deep bed of coals. Then, with the stage set for reverie, was the time to go down to the cache.

On one such night I picked a knot I knew well. A large one, it had come from a big lower branch of a pine that had grown by itself close to the shore of the little rock-bound lake where I had found the rest. That pine was a sapling when the first voyageurs came through on their trading-expeditions some three hundred years ago, was well grown at the time of the

American Revolution, crashed to earth during some storm before the loggers moved in sixty years ago. There it lay while the younger pines around it were harvested, and disintegrated slowly as the birch came in. Its knots survived a great fire that swept the area as an aftermath of the logging, lying there hidden beneath the duff and away from the heat.

I tucked the knot in among the glowing coals, where it was quietly caressed by exploring tongues of flame. It began to burn, gently at first, the yellows, blues, and reds of the resins bathing its black surface with strange lights. Here was the accumulated sunlight of bygone days giving off its warmth once more, the sun that had shone over the Quetico-Superior centuries before we were born. Now it was ours to share, and with it, all that the pine had known throughout its life. That pine knot was a concentration not only of energy but of the country itself. Burning it was the climax not only to its growth but to the expedition on which I found it.

CHAPTER 6

SMOKY GOLD

THE leaves are gone from the hillsides and the glory of the red maple and of the yellow aspen and birch is strewn upon the ground. Only in the protected swamps is there any color, the smoky gold of the tamaracks. A week ago those trees were yellow, but now they are dusty and tarnished. These are days of quietly falling needles when after each breath of wind the air is smoky with their drift.

I walked into a muskeg where they grew, a muskeg bedded deep with sphagnum and heather and where the ground trembled beneath me. Each tree showered me with tiny needles and the place where I stood became a golden carpet.

The tamaracks were all of a size, for thirty years ago the larch sawfly had killed all the old trees. Not a stand escaped and only rarely is it possible now to find any living relics of the past. In the center of the bog were a few old stubs, smooth and silvery gray but as sound as the day they had died. Those trees were good for winter nights if you wanted excitement in your fireplace. Tamarack burns with a fierce crackling and a constant barrage of spitting sparks. Here are character and individuality, a release from the cold acidity of the swamps where it was grown, a final flaunting of the energy stored under bitter conditions of existence. The tamarack matures slowly, is close-grained and tough, with fibers that are packed tightly with resins. When it burns, those pent-up stores of energy all but explode.

Not long ago I traveled through Illinois, Indiana, and Iowa, and there I found many small and isolated tamarack bogs no different from those in the north. There were the same trees with their undercover of bog plants, even the same birds and insects, the identical ecological community. These tiny relic areas—all that now remain of the forests that once were at the forefront of the glacial ice—survived intact when the great recession took place because the ground waters stayed cold and the acid peat that was their base did not change. They are islands of the past, tiny primitive areas that once were part of the ice age. They had seen the glaciers come and go and were ancient thousands of years before they were seen by man.

To me they appeared as remnants of a surviving race, tightly knit and isolated communities in the midst of a homogeneous conquering power. Constantly subjected to the influence of the invaders, they had survived because the conditions that gave them racial character had not changed.

Here was ecological integrity and fortitude, with survival due not so much to adaptation to the adversities of climate and competition as to the continuance of the basic temperatures and acidities of the bogs in which they grew. Human communities faced with the same desperate problem maintain their character by keeping alive the legendry and spiritual resources that have made them what they are. The tamaracks so far have not changed, nor have the other members of the bog community of which they are a part. The muskeg is the hard ecological core that makes survival possible. As long as the core remains constant, the character of the swamps will never change. Should it vary in the slightest, the engulfing influences of the surrounding country will spell their doom.

The tamaracks seem dedicated to the past, for they are not only relic communities but serve as storehouses of ancient vegetational history. Long before they began to grow, while the bogs that now protect them were glacial pools filling in with peat, these records were accumulating. Pollen grains from all the forests of the entire area were drifting over those pools in the spring, sifting down over the water, sinking into the cold acid peat. There they rested, layer upon layer, preserved perfectly in the order of their falling. By identifying these pollen grains, it is possible to reconstruct the phantom forests of the past. Beneath the golden carpet of tamarack needles around me was the story of every climatic change, every forest fire, every plant invasion up to the time the book was closed by the completion of the mat of sphagnum over the open water of the original bog.

This fall I was on the Island River. It was late October and the tamaracks were as golden as they would ever be. Before me was a stand of wild rice, yellow against the water, and because it was a bluebird day there was not a wing in the sky. I stood there just looking at the horizon. Suddenly the sun went under a cloud and it began to snow, softly at first, and then as the wind rose the serrated ranks of tamaracks across the bay almost disappeared in swirling flakes. A flock of northern bluebills tore out of the sky with that canvas-ripping sound that only bluebills make when they have been riding the tail of the wind and decide to come in. In a split second, an instant in which I was too startled even to move, there were a hundred wings where before there had been nothing but space. Then they were gone and in the same instant the sun came out.

Across the river the gold of the tamaracks was now covered with silver, the final display of the season. The snow would strip those branches bare, but I would remember that wild flurry of wings coming out of the storm, then the quiet and the sunlight and the silvered gold of the shoreline.

In the midwestern states, it is doubtful if the relic tamarack swamps can long survive the onslaught of the bulldozer and the ditching machine. They occupy, according to economists and land experts, far more space than they should, space that might well be converted into productive farmland. A little clearing of the worthless sphagnum and heather, a few cords of rather mediocre firewood, and a good straight ditch through the layer of black peat are all that is required. Then a sweetening of the acid soil and furrows will pave the way for worth-while production.

When they go, we will lose not only storage basins for water and final refuges for birds and wildlife, but museums of the past, examples to shifting humans of the stability of an ecological community that has stood the test of time. We will lose much of beauty if we trade them for more farmland, and we will lose our chance to study a primeval environment, its interrelationships and dependencies.

In the north there will no doubt always be tamarack swamps, for there the stands are extensive enough to survive and are a definite part of an ecological pattern that does not include agricultural land. Their smoky gold in late October will always be a benediction before the coming of the snows.

CHAPTER 7

THE LAST MALLARD

T HE hunting-seasons were over and the north lay quiet and still. No more cars with red-jacketed hunters roaring up and down the roads, no longer the sharp crack of high-powered rifles back in the hills. The country was alone at last and waiting for the snows, deer heading for the swamps, the ducks long ago gone south. There was

176

peace on the rocky ridges on either side of Madden Creek and it was good to be there just to listen and feel. Now the country belonged to me, all of it, for there was nothing there which anyone wanted—no game to kill, no fish to catch, nothing worth taking out.

For half a year it would lie there alone, frozen and white and undisturbed. The deer on sunny days would work out into its gullies and sometimes cross the ridges. The wolves would range its waterways and on moonlight nights they would howl from the tops of the hills. At dusk the horned owls would hoot from the darkness of the timber and northern lights would play the horizons with no one there to see.

For half a year the wilderness would return. It was for that reason I wanted to spend a day there, to get the feel of it after the violence had passed, to recapture the sense of wildness before the big snows made travel difficult. I wanted to know the breathlessness during the period of waiting which always comes at the time of freeze-up.

It was clear and still the morning I went in. Whisky-jacks were warbling softly and the chickadees seemed everywhere. A partridge burst out of an aspen thicket and zigzagged crazily through the trees. I climbed a ridge to get a better view of the valley. Below me was a long meadow of brown grass, the creek a ribbon of blue ice winding through it. A woodpecker hammered away at a dry stub, its sharp clatter echoing over the hills. I could hear the soft chuckle of running water, knew it meant one last open riffle before the creek entered the lake.

I climbed down the ridge and found a logging road along the creek bottom leading through a cedar swamp. Long ago someone had cut fence posts there, and a pile of them lay beside the trail. The posts were still hard and dry, silver gray with the weathering of half a century, sound as the day they were killed by a beaver dam down below. The cedar posts smelled good to me and there was a solid feel to them. I approved of such work. It was elemental and clean, in keeping with my mood and the character of the country.

Leaving the swamp, I climbed another ridge and stopped on top of a bare glaciated knob of granite overlooking the upper reaches of the meadow. Now I could see distinctly the riffle I had heard and a little pool of blue water just below it, a sliver of blue November sky caught in the vast brown net of the marsh. It was then I heard a sound that transformed the entire scene, a lone and resonant quack.

It was far away, but it startled me just the same, so out of place did it seem in that frozen creek bottom. I focused my glasses on the little pool and there I saw the mallard, a lone black swimming around sedately all by itself. Long ago it should have winged its way toward the south with the big V-shaped flocks while the lakes were still open and there was a chance to rest and feed. For some reason it had become separated from the rest, and when the cold settled down and there were fewer and fewer spots of open water, it had stayed on. Another night or two of zero weather with the little pool of open water growing smaller and smaller and one morning it would be frozen fast. Then a mink would find it, or a fox, or a coyote, and a few gorgeous wing feathers would mark the place where it had died.

For some time I remained motionless, watching the bird circling slowly around and around, but as I lay there I planned my strategy down to the minutest detail. Somehow I must flush that bird so it would fly toward the south, frighten it enough so that it would instinctively take the right direction. To throw a stone or flush it from a distance would not be enough; I must get close so that out of sheer panic it would really climb and not circle back to the pool. This would take stealth and finesse. Besides, I wanted to get close enough to see the sunlight on its wings as it took to the air, get the wild sense of desperate power as the bird made its last climb toward the sky.

I dropped to the smooth, hard surface of the ledge and slithered like a snake into the brush near by. Then, shedding my jacket, I crawled down an old deer trail closely hedged by aspen and birch and worked my way finally into the long, concealing grass of the creek bottom. There I lay quietly and caught up with my breathing. The tattoo of the pileated woodpecker was loud and insistent now, far too loud to suit me in the midst of my stalking. Once I caught a flash of black wings and red topknot as it flew directly over me to a stub across the creek. There it went to work again, its machine-gun racket deadening all other sounds.

The ground was frozen hard and the hummocks were just firm enough to make me crawl between them. Underneath me the grass, stiff with frost, crackled as I inched my way toward the pool. Ahead was a low windfall. For a time I studied it. If I had to crawl over, I would be in plain sight, and that would put an end to the game I was playing. The mallard was wary. They always are when alone and lost from the flocks. They have to be, in order to survive. When I reached the log, I raised my head to the level of its top and saw only oceans of brown grass. The log was cedar, hard and as silvery gray as those in the swamp. There was a smooth place between two branches just wide enough for me to slip through. Carefully I drew myself into the crotch, started to slide ahead, and stuck. My shirt gave way and I slid easily into the sedge on the other side.

Dangerously close now, I could hear the quacking plainly, even the soft splashing as the mallard dipped and fed. It was then I detected a slight note of alarm, just the faintest hint of uncertainty. For a long time I lay there almost fearing to breathe, ready for the wild quack of alarm and the furious beating of wings which would follow. Then the alarm note disappeared and I lay quietly, listening and watching. To accomplish my purpose, I must get much closer. The chance that the bird would fly in the right direction was a gamble under any conditions, but I had a strong hunch that if it was really frightened, it might in the excitement of the moment forget its old habits and head for the south and the open water not many miles away.

Once more I focused my glasses on the still unsuspecting bird, a beautiful black with touches of bronze along its sides, well fed and heavy, the blue-green of the wing bars shining in the sun. I knew where it had spent the fall: in the rice beds of Hula and along the Wind River and Back Bay, harvesting the rice the Indians had left. I watched it dip and feed, moving around that little pool as blithely as though there was no danger for a thousand miles.

A field mouse scurried past my nose and dove into a grassy burrow. For an instant I lay with my ear to the ground, listening to the tiny scurryings and rustlings as it worked itself into the jungle of grass stems.

It was then I became conscious of a great bulk lying directly across my path. Screened by grass, I saw the silvery gray of another huge cedar log. There was no way to get under it; again I would have to go over in plain view. I lay there studying that log as though it were a personal enemy, fallen there a century before to thwart me on this particular day.

Slowly I lifted myself again between two stubs, got caught again just as before, carefully released the fold of my shirt, and began to slide through. Then a branch snapped with an ear-splitting crack and the pool became alive as the mallard took to the air. I jumped to the top of the log, shouted and waved my arms, stumbled down to the pool, and made as much commotion as possible.

The bird climbed high, then swung to the north toward Wind Bay and some of the potholes where it used to feed. Just as the lone speck was disappearing over the horizon, it turned, came directly back, made a high circle over the pool, saw me there waving my arms, and then headed straight toward the sun and the south. I stood watching it disappearing into the haze. In a few hours, if it would only keep on, it would be down where there was open water and the flocks still feeding.

It was late when I reached the cabin, and the sky was rosy with the sunset. For a last afternoon I had been a wilderness hunter, had feasted my eyes on a great brown swamp and a frozen river, had listened to a rapids and talked to the whisky-jacks and chickadees. I had been an inspector of fence posts and had made the acquaintance of a field mouse. But, far more important than all of these, I had watched a last mallard climb into the sky and seen it head for the south.

Thoreau was at my side that night. "We should come home from afar," he told me, "from adventures and perils and discoveries every day, with new experiences and character."

CHAPTER 8

NORTHERN LIGHTS

T HE lights of the aurora moved
and shifted over the horizon. Sometimes there were shafts
of yellow tinged with green, then masses of evanescence
which moved from east to west and back again. Great streamers of bluish white zigzagged like a tremendous trembling curtain from one end of the sky to the other. Streaks of yellow

and orange and red shimmered along the flowing borders. Never for a moment were they still, fading until they were almost completely gone, only to dance forth again in renewed splendor with infinite combinations and startling patterns of design.

The lake lay like a silver mirror before me, and from its frozen surface came subterranean rumblings, pressure groans, sharp reports from the newly forming ice. As far as I could see, the surface was clear and shining. That ice was something to remember here in the north, for most years the snows come quickly and cover the first smooth glaze of freezing almost as soon as it is formed, or else the winds ruffle the surface of the crystallizing water and fill it with ridges and unevenness. But this time there had been no wind or snow to interfere, and the ice everywhere was clear—seven miles of perfect skating, something to dream about in years to come.

Hurriedly I strapped on my skates, tightened the laces, and in a moment was soaring down the path of shifting light which stretched endlessly before me. Out in the open away from shore there were few cracks—stroke—stroke—stroke—long and free, and I knew the joy that skating and skiing can give, freedom of movement beyond myself. But to get the feel of soaring, there must be miles of distance and conditions must be right. As I sped down the lake, I was conscious of no effort, only of the dancing lights in the sky and a sense of lightness and exaltation.

Shafts of light shot up into the heavens above me and concentrated there in a final climactic effort in which the shifting colors seemed drained from the horizons to form one gigantic rosette of flame and yellow and greenish purple. Suddenly I grew conscious of the reflections from the ice itself and that I was skating through a sea of changing color caught between the streamers above and below. At that moment I was part of the aurora, part of its light and of the great curtain that trembled above me.

Those moments of experience are rare. Sometimes I have known them while swimming in the moonlight, again while paddling a canoe when there was no wind and the islands seemed inverted and floating on the surface. I caught it once when the surf was rolling on an ocean coast and I was carried on the crest of a wave that had begun a thousand miles away. Here it was once more—freedom of movement and detachment from the earth.

Down the lake I went straight into the glistening path, speeding through a maze of changing color—stroke—stroke—stroke—the ringing of steel on ice, the sharp, reverberating rumbles of expansion below. Clear ice for the first time in years, and the aurora blazing away above it.

At the end of the lake I turned and saw the glittering lights of Winton far behind me. I lay down on the ice to rest. The sky was still bright and I watched the shifting lights come and go. I knew what the astronomers and the physicists said, that they were caused by sunspots and areas of gaseous disturbance on the face of the sun that bombarded the earth's stratosphere with hydrogen protons and electrons which in turn exploded atoms of oxygen, nitrogen, helium, and the other elements surrounding us. Here were produced in infinite combinations all the colors of the spectrum. It was all very plausible and scientific, but tonight that explanation left me cold. I was in no mood for practicality, for I had just come skating down the skyways themselves and had seen the aurora from the inside. What did the scientists know about what I had done? How could they explain what had happened to me and the strange sensations I had known?

Much better the poem of Robert Service telling of the great beds of radium emanating shafts of light into the northern darkness of the Yukon and how men went mad trying to find them. How infinitely more satisfying to understand and feel the great painting by Franz Johnson of a lone figure crossing a muskeg at night with the northern lights blazing above it. I stood before that painting in the Toronto Art Gallery one day and caught all the stark loneliness, all the beauty and the cold of that scene, and for a moment forgot the busy city outside.

I like to think of them as the ghost dance of the Chippewas. An Indian once told me that when a warrior died, he gathered with his fellows along the northern horizon and danced the war dances they had known on earth. The shifting streamers and the edgings of color came from the giant headdresses they wore. I was very young when I first saw them that way, and there were times during those enchanted years when I thought I could distinguish the movements of individual bodies as they rushed from one part of the sky to another. I knew nothing then of protons or atoms and saw the northern lights as they should be seen. I knew, too, the wonderment that only a child can know and a beauty that is enhanced by mystery.

As I lay there on the ice and thought of these things I wondered if legendry could survive scientific truth, if the dance of the protons would replace the ghost dance of the Chippewas. I wondered as I began to skate toward home if anything—even knowing the physical truth—could ever change the beauty of what I had seen, the sense of unreality. Indian warriors, exploding atoms, beds of radium—what difference did it make? What counted was the sense of the north they gave me, the fact that they typified the loneliness, the stark beauty of frozen muskegs, lakes, and forests. Those northern lights were part of me and I of them.

On the way back I noticed that there was a half-moon over the cluster of lights in the west. I skirted the power dam at the mouth of the Kawishiwi River, avoiding the blaze of its light on the black water below the spillway. Then suddenly the aurora was gone and the moon as well.

Stroke—stroke—stroke—the shores were black now, pinnacled spruce and shadowed birch against the sky. At the landing I looked back. The ice was still grumbling and groaning, still shaping up to the mold of its winter bed.

WINTER

CHAPTER I

COMING OF THE SNOW

THE earth is rigid, the water-
ways are hard and blue. Aspen and birch are bare traceries
against the sky, spruce and pine dark masses against the mauve
of the hills. Hollows are deep in leaves. They are damp, and
smell of wetness and the beginning of mold. There is a sense
of expectancy, a waiting and a breathlessness. The rustling

sounds are gone, the scurryings and small, dry movements of fall. There is a hush, a deep and quiet breathing after the hurried and colored violence of the months just gone. Birds are moving and squirrels storing the last of their winter's food. The ice on the lakes has secured the shores and islands, has adjusted itself to the form it must keep until spring. The woods are ready, and as the zero hour approaches, an even greater silence settles down over the north.

There is a moment of suspense when the quiet can be felt, when it presses down on everything and to speak seems a ·sacrilege. Suddenly the air is white with drifting flakes and the tension is gone. Down they come, settling on the leaves, into crevices in bark, on the lichen-covered rocks, disintegrating immediately into more and more wetness. Then almost magically the ground is no longer brown but speckled with white. Now there is an infinitesimal rustling as the flakes drift into the leaves and duff. Swiftly the whiteness spreads, then the earth is sealed and autumn is gone.

Now there is great activity among the birds and squirrels. Chickadees, nuthatches, and pine siskins are everywhere. Squirrels race madly to finish their belated harvest. There is new excitement in the air, a feeling of release. Life will now be lived in an established white world where conditions of food and shelter will not change for a long time. Stability has come to the north and to my own life as well.

The coming of the snow adds zest to my activities. Now there will be time for a multitude of things that during the feverish moving about of summer and fall were denied me, leisure after the long and constant busyness. To me that is the real meaning of the first snowfall—not a cessation of effort, but a drawing of the curtain on so many of the warm-weather activities that consume so much time. The snow means a return to a world of order, peace, and simplicity. Those first drifting flakes are a benediction and the day on which they come is different from any other in the year.

One morning after this first heavy snowfall I took to the woods. The temperature was down, the snow deep and drifted where the wind had gone. No longer were the grasses showing or the long, sere stems of weeds. Logs and stumps and low-growing shrubs were now completely covered and the ground was smooth and white. Balsams and spruces were heavily laden and some of the birches were bending low. There was no track of any kind, not a sign of life in the frozen stillness around me.

As the sun came over the ridge, it changed the snow and its purple shadows to sparkling silver. The temperature was zero and the trees were crisp and starched with frost. There was no sound but the soft *swish-swish* of the snowshoes and the creaking of the thongs as I broke the trail.

On the sunny side of a ridge I stopped to rest, for the snow was deep and not well packed. There I discovered that I was not alone. A blue jay flew across an opening before me, a streak of blue flame against the glistening white. He perched in an aspen near by where I could admire his black highwayman's mask, his black and white wing bars, his vivid, icy blue. He gave his hard, brazen call, more of a challenge than a song, a challenge to the storm and cold. There was jauntiness and fortitude, announcing to me and to the whole frozen world that where there is wine and sparkle in the air, it is joy to be alive. I liked that jay and what he stood for; no softness there, pure hardiness and disregard of the elements.

A flock of pine siskins dashed into the spruce tops and scurried around busily, exploring the cones for seeds. Black-capped chickadees were also high in the trees where they could catch the first warming rays of the sun. How merry they all were and full of life and song!

A little farther on a red squirrel scolded me from a pine stub. His twin tracks led from beneath a log, where he had been sleeping during the storm. He was out now to find the pine cones he had buried so carefully in the leaves and duff before the coming of the snow. He would find some of them, but not all—and thereby live up to his name as the greatest forester in the north, the largest planter of pine trees on the continent. He wasn't quite sure what to make of me, stomping his feet, chattering and scolding, looking me over first from one side of the stub and then from the other. When I didn't move, he came down head first, a jerk at a time, poised for a moment wide-eyed and alert just above me, and then with a wild flurry of tail dove for his hole.

Down in the valley I saw the tracks of a snowshoe rabbit, just a short track leading from one white-mounded windfall to another. A longer excursion in the heavy snow might have been dangerous, for now the great horned owl was hunting every night, watching the unbroken white for any sign of movement. Although the snowshoe hare is white, his black eyes give him away. He is wise to stay under cover until the snow packs or until some bright moonlit night lures him recklessly into the open.

I left the hills and headed for the cedar swamp down below. There I found the deer tracks I expected, heading for the protection of the lowlands. Along the well-beaten trails they would make, the deer would feed on the low-hanging cedar that is their winter food. By spring there would be a distinct browse line as high as they could reach, not only in the swamps but along the shoreline of every lake and pond. So important is the cedar as winter food that it is often the determining factor in survival.

Along the edge of the swamp a partridge exploded out of a drift, burst like a bomb within a foot of my snowshoes, and flew into the top of a tall aspen, where it proceeded to bud as unconcernedly as though this was the normal way of getting out of bed. Survival in the cold is simple for the grouse. Long ago they must have learned that down and snow mean warmth. The only trouble with the plan was that foxes and coyotes and weasels knew it too, knew where to pounce at the ends of the short trails leading into the drifts.

A little muskeg lay below me, a place where the cranberries grew and their long, delicate vines interlaced the sphagnum. The hummocks were covered and the entire surface of the bog was smooth as any floor. Beneath that surface was a jungle of grassy roots and stems, tiny mountains of sphagnum, forests of heather, the whole interwoven with thousands of twisting burrows of meadow mice. They would not see the sun for months, would live in a shadowy blue and white translucency, safe from storms and hawks and owls. Only the weasels could follow them there and sometimes the probing nose of a fox. Theirs was a world removed, an intricate winter community, self-sufficient and well organized.

Life had changed for every living thing in the north. Mating and nesting and the rearing of young were over. There was only one great problem for all: how to survive the deep snows and the long, bitter cold. For some the answer was sleep, with stored fat the source of energy and warmth. For others there was still the constant and never ending search for food and shelter.

It is true that simplicity and order had come to the wilderness and a quiet that the months since spring had never known. There was joy and beauty in the winter woods, but there was also suffering and death. Only the strong would survive to bear their young in the spring, but this was the way it had always been. All forms of life prepared for it, accepted the new austere environment without panic.

The blue jay called again and I caught one brilliant glimpse as he flashed beneath the trees. Gay and cocksure as ever, he had no cares or worries as to his place in the wilderness picture. For him there was no calm resignation or concern with peace. Whether or not he survived today, this moment he would tell the world what he thought and challenge all comers, including the snow and the cold.

CHAPTER 2

WILDERNESS MUSIC

Last night I followed a ski trail into the Lucky Boy Valley. It was dark and still, and the pines and spruces there almost met overhead. During the day it had snowed, and the festooned trees were vague massed drifts against the stars. Breathless after my run, I stopped to rest and listen. In that snow-cushioned place there was no sound, no wind moaning in the branches, no life or movement of any kind.

As I stood there leaning on my sticks, I thought of Jack Linklater, a Scotch-Cree of the Hudson's Bay Company. In such a place he would have heard the music, for he had a feeling for the "wee" people and for many things others did not understand. Sometimes when we were on the trail together he would ask me to stop and listen, and when I could not hear he would laugh. Once in a stand of quaking aspen in a high place when the air was full of their whispering, he dropped his pack and stood there, a strange and happy light in his eyes. Another time, during the harvesting of wild rice when the dusk was redolent with the parching fires on the shores of Hula Lake, he called me to him, for he felt that somehow I must hear the music too.

"Can't you hear it now?" he said. "It's very plain tonight."

I stood there with him and listened, but heard nothing, and as I watched the amused and somewhat disappointed look on his face I wondered if he was playing a game with me. That time he insisted that he could hear the sound of women's and children's voices and the high quaver of an Indian song, though we were far from the encampment. Now that the years have passed and Jack has gone to the Happy Hunting Grounds, I believe that he actually heard something and that the reason I could not was that this was music for Indians and for those whose ears were attuned.

One night we were camped on the Maligne River in the Quetico on a portage trail used for centuries by Indians and voyageurs. The moon was full, and the bowl below the falls was silver with mist. As we sat listening to the roar of Twin Falls, there seemed to be a sound of voices of a large party making the carry. The sound ebbed and swelled in volume with the ebb and flow of the plunging water. That night I thought I heard them, too, and Jack was pleased. Wilderness music? Imagination? I may never know, but this much I do know from traveling with Jack: he actually heard something, and those who have lived close to nature all of their lives are sensitive to many things lost to those in the cities.

We send out costly expeditions to record the feelings, expressions, and customs of primitive tribes untouched by civilization, considering such anthropological research to be worth while because it gives us an inkling of why we moderns behave as we do. We recognize that a great deal has been lost to us during the so-called civilized centuries—intuitive awarenesses that primitives still possess. Children still have them, but they soon disappear. Some individuals retain them as long as they live. All, however, have a need and hunger for them, and much of the frustration and boredom we experience is no doubt due to our inability to recapture these forgotten ways of perception.

While most of us are too far removed to hear the wilderness music that Jack Linklater heard, there are other forms—not so subtle, perhaps, but still capable of bringing to our consciousness the same feelings that have stirred human kind since the beginning of time. Who is not stirred when the wild geese go by, when the coyotes howl on a moonlit night, or when the surf crashes against the cliffs? Such sounds have deep appeal because they are associated with the background of the race. Why does the rhythmic tom-tom beat of drums affect us? Because it, too, is primitive and was part of our heritage centuries before music as we know it now was ever conceived. Wilderness music to me is any sound that brings to mind the wild places I have known.

Once during a long absence from the north I heard the call of a loon, the long, rollicking laughter that in the past I had heard echoing across the wild reaches of the Quetico lakes. It was in Tennessee that I heard it, but the instant I caught the first long wail, chills of gladness chased themselves up and down my spine. For a long time I stood there and listened, but I did not hear it again. While I waited, the north came back to me with a rush and visions of wilderness lakes and rivers crowded upon me. I saw the great birds flying into the sunsets, groups of them playing over the waters of Lac la Croix, Kawnipi, and Batchewaung. I saw the reaches of Saganaga in the early morning, a camp on some lonely island with the day's work done and nothing to do but listen and dream. And then in the recesses of my mind the real calling began as it had a thousand times in the past, the faintest hint of an echo from over the hills, answered before it died by a closer call and that in turn by another until the calling of the loons from all the lakes around blended in a continuous symphony.

There were other times that also came back to me, times when the clouds were dark and the waves rolling high, when the calling reached a pitch of madness which told of coming storm; mornings when the sun was bright and happy laughter came from the open water; nights when one lone call seemed to embody all the misery and tragedy in the world. I knew as I stood there waiting that when once a man had known that wild and eery calling and lost himself in its beauty, should he ever hear a hint of it again, no matter where he happened to be, he would have a vision of the distance and freedom of the north.

One day in the south of England I was walking through a great beech wood on an old estate near Shrivenham. There was a little brook flowing through the woods, and its gurgle as it ran through a rocky dell seemed to accentuate my sense of the age of those magnificent trees. I was far from home, as far away from the wilderness of the north as I had ever been. Those great trees were comforting to me even though I knew that just beyond them was open countryside.

Then suddenly I heard a sound that changed everything: a soft nasal twang from high in the branches, the call of a nuthatch. Instantly that beech grove was transformed into a stand of tall, stately pines; the brown beech leaves on the ground became a smooth carpet of golden needles, and beyond this cared-for forest were rugged ridges and deep, timbered valleys, roaring rivers and placid lakes, with a smell of resin and duff in the sun. The call of the nuthatch had done all that, had given me a vision of the wilderness as vivid as though for the moment I had actually been there.

How satisfying to me are the sounds of a bog at night! I like to paddle into a swampy bay in the lake country and just sit there and listen to the slow sloshing-around of moose and deer, the sharp pistol crack of a beaver tail slapping the water, the guttural, resonant pumping of a bittern. But the real music of a bog is the frog chorus. If they are in full swing when you approach, they stop by sections as though part of the orchestra was determined to carry on in spite of the faintheartedness of the rest. One must sit quietly for some time before they regain their courage. At first there are individual piping notes, a few scattered guttural croaks, then a confused medley as though the instruments were being tuned. Finally in a far corner a whole section swings into tremulous music, hesitant at the start but gradually gathering momentum and volume. Soon a closer group begins, and then they all join in until there is again a sustained and grand crescendo of sound.

This is a primeval chorus, the sort of wilderness music which reigned over the earth millions of years ago. That sound floated across the pools of the carboniferous era. You can still hear it in the Everglades: the throaty, rasping roar of the alligators and, above that, the frightened calls and screams of innumerable birds. One of the most ancient sounds on earth, it is a continuation of music from the past, and, no matter where I listen to a bog at night, strange feelings stir within me.

One night in the south of Germany I was walking along the River Main at Frankfurt. It was spring and sunset. Behind me were the stark ruins of the city, the silhouettes of broken walls and towers, the horrible destruction of the bombing. Across the river was a little village connected with the city by the broken span of a great bridge. In the river were the rusting hulls of barges and sunken boats. The river gurgled softly around them and around the twisted girders of the blown-up span. It was a scene of desolation and sadness.

Then I was conscious of a sound that was not of the war, the hurrying whisper of wings overhead. I turned, and there against the rosy sky was a flock of mallards. I had forgotten that the river was a flyway, that there were still such delightful things as the sound of wings at dusk, rice beds yellowing in the fall, and the soft sound of quacking all through the night. A lone flock of mallards gave all that to me, awoke a thousand memories as wilderness music always does.

There are many types of music, each one different from the rest: a pack of coyotes and the wild, beautiful sound of them as they tune up under the moon; the song of a white-throated sparrow, its one clear note so closely associated with trout streams that whenever I hear one, I see a sunset-tinted pool and feel the water around my boots. The groaning and cracking of forming ice on the lakes, the swish of skis or snowshoes in dry snow—wilderness music, all of it, music for Indians and for those who have ears to hear.

CHAPTER 3

TRAPPER'S CABIN

THE cabin on Snowbank Lake was primitive; the unpeeled logs were chinked with moss; there was no floor and only one small window. The cabin faded into the tall black spruces around it as if it had always been there. It smelled of balsam, for in one corner was a bunk full of the resinous tips and on the packed dirt floor needles were the pattern.

The cabin had not been built for summer comfort or view.

It had no real-estate value. It had one purpose only: to give shelter at the end of a long day on the trap lines, shelter from the gales of winter when the snow was deep and the cold enough to sear a man's lungs.

Even for a trapper's cabin it was small, just big enough for a man and his outfit, a tiny stove, a corner table, and the bunk; there were hand-whittled pegs for clothes and packs, a narrow shelf below the window. But at night when the trees cracked with the frost and the bitter wind whipped the unprotected shore, it was as cozy and warm as a bear's den under a windfall. The roof was low, and the rafters stuck far out from the eaves as though the builder had forgotten to trim them. Those eaves gave the cabin the effect of squatting low beneath the trees, and made it as much a part of the forest floor as a moss-covered boulder or a hummock cushioned with duff. Only a few spruce had been cut for the logs, and with the passing years the little gap had been filled with new growth until there seemed to be no perceptible break between the roof and the low-hanging branches of the trees.

When I entered that cabin I was close to the wild. Here life was primitive and I felt as Thoreau did when he said: "Drive life into a corner and reduce it to its simplest terms." Here, if anywhere, was the simplicity he meant. This was no place for fancy or unnecessary equipment. The cabin meant moccasins, rough wool, and leather—and simple thoughts. The complicated problems of society, politics, war and peace seemed far removed. The only thoughts that thrived here were of squirrels and birds and snowshoe trails. Here I felt as much a part of the out-of-doors as when sleeping under a ledge.

I liked to lie in the balsam bunk and look up at the pole rafters and study the deer-mouse nest in one corner and the lichen and fungi that had taken hold on the rough logs. As the cabin became warm, the mouse thawed out; a slight rustling and suddenly big transparent ears and bright black eyes emerged from the nest. For a long time the little animal would watch me and when convinced that I was harmless, would come down to the table to pick up crumbs.

Sometimes a red squirrel came in through a hole under the eaves. Again the long contemplation and final acceptance. He and I were partners, in a sense—my part to leave something on the table, his to make me feel that I belonged.

This could not happen in a modern mouseproof cabin, and what a pity it is! I have always felt that cabins belong to the animals of the woods as much as they do to us and that the animals should feel as much at home in them as though there were no doors or walls. By shutting them out, we lose their companionship and the feeling of trust which comes only when the barriers of strangeness and fear are overcome.

Sometimes at night I would waken and listen to the tips of the spruce branches rubbing against the walls, caressing them softly. That cabin was still part of the living forest, would eventually be part of the moss and duff again. At such times my thoughts seemed to merge with the trees and the sound of their movement in the wind, their creaking and moaning as they rubbed against one another. It satisfied a longing for closeness to a primitive environment, the hunger to return for a little while to the wilderness. Centuries of caves, of shelters under the trees, of dry spots beneath ledges and windfalls, of listening to the sounds of the night have left their mark. The Snowbank cabin was part of all that.

Another cabin that gave me this feeling was on the Sand River south of my home. It, too, was of logs, but roofed with wide strips of birchbark anchored with stones. The rafters were wide enough in their overlap to shelter a woodpile underneath, an ax, a saw, and other gear, generous enough to heal the break between the walls and the ground. The cabin made a picture squatting there on its little spit of land commanding a view up and down the river. On one side spruces and balsams hedged it closely, but the other side was snuggled close against a great gray rock out of reach of the wind. The trapper who built it may have thought it was just another shelter, but, far more than that, it was a picture in logs and rock which gave pleasure to all who passed. He was probably more of an artist than he knew, unable to resist the view up and down the river, the sunrises and sunsets, and the sound of whistling wings as mallards flew over on their way to the rice beds beyond.

Charley Raney's Stony River cabin was surrounded by high hills, but you could hear the whisper of the river as it flowed across the boulders down below. Here was not only primitiveness, but isolation in a wild and glorious setting. That cabin reminded me of cabins in the Austrian Tyrol, isolated little shelters perched on inaccessible crags reached only by steep mountain trails. There were no sunsets because the dusk settled swiftly between the hills, no vistas, no sense of space—as wild and lonely a place as the bottom of a canyon, and Charley Raney, the mad trapper who built it, found there a mystery and wildness that complemented his own nature. I sometimes wondered how mad he was—whether he was not saner than many who passed judgment upon him. He loved to sit on his stoop and play his violin to the accompaniment of the rapids. He was as much a part of his setting as the Sibelius he loved was part of the forests and lakes of Finland.

There are many trappers' cabins in the north and there are many mansions called cabins. Many of them are comfortable and beautiful in their way, but when I enter them there is no change for me, merely an extension of civilized living away from the towns. Motor boats, highways, and planes make them as accessible as suburban homes. I find no sense of seclusion or solitude in them, for their conveniences carry with them the associations and responsibilities of urban living. Sometimes they are so comfortable, so removed from all physical effort, that they nullify the real purpose of going to the woods: doing primitive things in primitive ways and recapturing simplicity.

Trappers' cabins are as natural as tents or teepees. They are part of the solitudes and as much a part of the wilderness as the trees and rocks themselves. In those cabins the wilderness always sings. Each time that deer mouse came to feed, I caught a single elfin note. I heard it on the Sand River one stormy night when the drifting snow was full of the sound of wings, and on the Stony when Charley's violin blended with the music of the rapids so closely that I could not tell them apart and I knew he was feeling not only the scene around him but the wilds and hinterlands of Europe's north.

CHAPTER 4

DARK HOUSE

I‌T was just ten years ago that Bob came home to catch the feeling of the Minnesota-Ontario border country in midwinter. He wanted, above all, to sit in a dark house with me again and watch the circling decoy and the scene below the ice. He wanted time to think long thoughts and hear the whispering of the snow outside the thin tarpaper walls. He wanted the good feeling that he used to know at night after a long day on skis and perhaps the taste of a fish fresh from the icy waters of the lakes of the north.

So one morning in January, though it was twenty below, we took off for the old haunts. The ski harnesses creaked as we pushed across the lower reaches of Fall Lake. Smoke rose straight above the chimneys in the little town of Winton at the end of the road and the sun dogs blazed over the horizon. It was far too cold to travel slowly. We pushed hard on our sticks, and the skis hissed over the powder-dry snow. We were the only ones abroad, the only ones foolish enough to be outside when we did not have to be. Still, fresh deer tracks crossed the lake, and on the portage into Cedar there were signs of rabbits, weasels, and mice.

A tiny tarpaper shack off the end of a long point was our goal. A friend had set it up weeks ago, told us where the spear was cached and the wooden decoy. For its use, we were to bring him a fish. That meant we had to take two. We shoveled the snow away from the door, fanned a flame to life in the little stove, and dug the spear and the decoy out of a drift.

Six inches of ice had to be cut out of the hole. We filled the coffeepot, closed the door, and settled down to wait. Outside the wind howled, but the little shelter was cozy and warm. At first we could see nothing but the green translucent water, but gradually our vision cleared and we could see farther and farther into the depths, finally to the very bottom itself. Light streamed through the snow and ice, and the bottom all but glowed.

In our field of vision were several whitish rocks and bits of shell, important landmarks of the scene. Soon eel grass and feathery milfoil emerged in the half-light, weaving slowly in the slight current of the narrows. The rocks and shells became as familiar as though we had been watching them for weeks, the tufts of waving grass as outstanding as trees in a meadow. In one corner was a clam, its narrow furrow distinct and sharp in the sand. A shaft of light angled over our hunting-ground, light reflected through flashing prisms of ice. The stage was set for action. This was worth the cold trek out, compensation for weeks of waiting; it was a scene of stark beauty and suspense such as the most elaborate stage setting never attained.

The spear rested easily against the inside edge of the ice, its handle free and ready to grasp, a cord fastened to Bob's wrist. Occasionally he shifted the point of a tine before it became too firmly embedded in its notch, twisted it slightly so that when the great moment came there would be no resistance, no wrenching free, nothing to interfere with the thrust. When the time came, the strike must be made with lightning speed.

I played the decoy, a six-inch model of a sucker minnow replete with fins and tail of shining tin. Whittled from a piece of cedar, it was weighted with lead and hung from the end of a string. Its tail was set so that with each motion of my hand it made wide and beautiful circles all around the hole.

As the coffee began to simmer, we shed outer jackets and mitts. Outside, it was still close to twenty below and the snow was whispering as Bob had hoped. After an hour of tension we began to relax, talked quietly about many things. A fish house is a fine place for visiting—not for arguments or weighty ideas, but rather for small talk, local politics and gossip, things we had seen coming in, ideas that required no effort, short simple thoughts that came as easily as breathing. This was no place for the expounding of strong, heady beliefs; such ideas need room and space in which to grow and expand. Furthermore, our energies must be conserved for the moment when the flash of a silver side below would eclipse everything else in the world.

"A northern pike will taste pretty good tonight," I said.

"Would taste pretty good," was Bob's reply.

"We'll clean it before it freezes," I said. "Save us the job when we get home."

"See that clam?" said Bob. "It's moving toward the outside of the hole. Getting out of the way while there's time."

"Those deer tracks this morning looked as though they'd been chased. Twenty feet at a jump for a while."

"Heading for the cedar on the south shore, really makin' time."

The small talk went on and on, and after a while there was nothing more to say and we lapsed into quiet, just sat and stared into the hole, watching the rhythmic turns of the little decoy, back and forth, around and around, its metal fins flashing in the light. After a time our vision blended with the bottom itself and we began to feel as though we were a part of the subterranean world below us, part of the clean sand, the white rocks, the waving eel grass. We became intimately familiar with each irregularity of the bottom, the ripple marks, the moving habits of each blade of grass, the air bubbles at the edge of the ice, even the shadows of clouds drifting by outside. Two hours went by and our senses all but fused with the blue-green environment below.

Then when we had begun to feel as though nothing could ever change, as though we might have been sitting in that same position for years, a gray torpedo-like shape slipped swiftly into the open and the static little world we had created exploded before our eyes. The grasses waved erratically, the white rocks disappeared, the water roiled.

The spear! screamed everything within us. Slowly—so slowly—cramped senses became aware, muscles began to move. As in a dream, fingers tightened around the cold, heavy steel; the point, withdrawn from its icy notch, hung poised, ready to strike. Directly below lay the gray shape of a great northern pike, its fins and tail moving slowly, its gill covers opening and closing with barely perceptible motion.

"Now!" came the shout, and suddenly the spear plunged downward, and in a violent instant the water boiled and the fish, the rocks, and the weeds disappeared in a green-white turmoil of confusion.

The spear and the fish came out of the hole in a cascade of water. I pushed out the door and we stumbled outside into the brilliant dazzle of sunlight on the snow, shouting, laughing at our good fortune, pounding each other on the back. This was a pinnacle of experience, and during that instant it seemed that few triumphs in the world of men could compare with it.

The pike stopped its thrashing at last and began to stiffen in the cold. We stepped back through the little door into quiet and darkness once more.

Finally the water cleared, and we could now see fresh scales on the bottom. The eel grass and milfoil were waving once more, and there again were the identical rocks and the whitened bits of shell. Even the clam was in the same position, working its way slowly toward the outside perimeter of our field. It seemed impossible that things could be the same after the violent eruption of a short time ago. But nothing had changed at all—a few more air bubbles under the ice, the scattered scales on the sand. Again the rhythmic turns of the decoy, around and around and around, its silver fins flashing in the light. The spear point wore itself down into another icy notch.

"That's one," said Bob. "That one goes to the house."

"The next one is ours," I answered, "the one we'll clean for supper."

Again the scene became familiar, and soon we were through talking, just sitting there watching and waiting as men have watched and waited since the beginning of time. The drifting snow whispered and swirled around our little house.

A shadow crossed one corner and the waving grasses trembled slightly, bowed gently toward the movement, came back to their old positions. The spear was loosened from its notch. At that moment the whole civilized world moved back to where it belonged, faded into a background that was nothing compared to the tremendous event taking place before our eyes. The grasses trembled as though expecting something to happen. The water itself seemed charged.

Then the shadow returned and a great pike lay directly below us, so close and so real that our numbed senses could not grasp what had actually happened. Its fins were moving slowly, its gills opening and closing. It lay there quietly looking at the decoy quivering at the end of its string.

The spear was withdrawn and with a single movement plunged into the water. Again the white and green turmoil, the open door and the sunshine.

We had enough, one for the house and one for our supper. We cached the spear and decoy, closed the door, and started off for home. It was a little warmer now and the skis slid smoothly over the trail we had made that morning. The west was orange and mauve and apple green, and the birches shone silver in the last level rays of the sun. By the time we reached the portage it was dusk and the afterglow burned behind the black masses of pine and spruce.

When we reached Fall Lake we could see the lights of the village at the end of the bay. Smoke still rose straight above the chimneys. With the dark it would be twenty below again, and in the morning the sun dogs would be out. The ice would soon be thick over the hole we had cut, and the tarpaper shack would be cold and dark. The grasses would tremble on the bottom, and the clam would plow its furrow unseen and undisturbed.

CHAPTER 5

THE RIVER

I TOOK the trail to the river because I wanted to see open water again after nothing but solid ice on the lakes, brittle frozen brush, and snow that felt like sand. I wanted to see something moving and alive and listen to the gurgle of water as it rippled its way around the rocks of some open place that had never quite closed. I knew

216

of such a place where in the summertime a rapids whitened the blue of the South Kawishiwi.

The snow was unbroken, and the jack pines were so heavily laden that their branches touched the ground. Not a sign of life anywhere until I approached the river and saw the delicate twin tracks of a weasel weaving in and out of the underbrush. The tracks disappeared at the base of a protruding stub—gateway, I knew, to the jungle of grass and duff underneath and the meadow mice that lived there. Then for twenty feet there was no sign until the tracks emerged through a tiny hole in the snow and continued on in a straight line to the open water.

I skied to the very edge of the riffle and stood there, feasting my eyes and ears. Moving water after thirty or forty below when the whole world had seemed a frozen crystal of blue and white was an exciting thing. The river was alive and every thing within it was alive. Bronze nuggets of gravel moved in the sunlight, and among them danced iridescent bits of shell, whirling madly for a moment only to settle and dance again. Sand eddied impatiently around the larger rocks, and as I watched I knew that, while all life now seemed dead beneath the surface, nothing had really changed. The river moved, blood still ran hot, and the endless cycle went on as before.

Now I caught an undertone beneath the gurgle of flowing water, the constant *swish-swish* of drifting ice and snow from the mass crowding the pool from above in a vain attempt to close the open blue wound in that vast unbroken surface of white. Some night at forty below the ice might win, and then there would be no open riffle until the spring.

It was then I saw the weasel standing on a log just below me. Snake-like in shape, this tiny bit of venom was less than a foot in length. Totally white with a faint tinge of yellow, the only contrast the jet-black tip of its tail and its beady eyes, the little animal watched me intently. Then it ran out to the end of the log extending into the water and stood there with one foot uplifted as though wondering whether to plunge in and make it to the other side or retrace its steps and face me.

I sucked softly on the back of my hand, making a sound like the squeak of a meadow mouse. Instantly it turned and looked at me long and steadily, a picture of perfect control and poise. Again I squeaked. Throwing caution to the winds, the weasel dove for the end of the log and in a moment was circling the place where I stood.

How impossible for any small creature to escape such speed and fluid grace, how hopeless to try and run from those smoothly rippling muscles, those sharp black eyes! Suddenly the weasel popped out from under a windfall within a foot of the end of my skis and gave me a wholly malevolent look as though knowing of my deception; then in a flash it was speeding down a fresh rabbit runway through the alders.

Mustela cicognani, the little killer, afraid of nothing ten times its size. I had once seen one attach itself to the throat of a partridge and hang on, biting and chewing through feathers and skin, while the bird climbed high above the trees. I saw the doomed bird plummet to the snow with the weasel still holding on, and while it drank its fill of the hot blood, it defied me. There the spirit of all predators, the epitome of speed and grace, deadly concentration, and an audacity born of the instinctive knowledge that there were no enemies to fear. There is poetry in the way a weasel can flow through a maze of branches and grass—the liquid movement, the perfect control that enables it to live off those less agile than itself.

Ermine, the mark of royalty: white pelts dotted with black tail tips, for centuries the hallmark of those who ruled. How thrilling my boyhood trap lines, the excitement of coming to a set and finding there a tiny frozen form! No compassion then, no feeling of sympathy for the hurt and suffering I had caused; merely wonder at having taken something so beautiful. What pure delight to feel the soft fur! I used to fondle the skins, knew the history of each and every one, became so attached to them that I actually hated to sell them at the end of the season. Far more than the actual worth of the fur on the market was what they meant to me. When I touched those wild furs I somehow made contact with a life that had nothing to do with home or school or parents. I was in a world of my own, a free and beautiful world where all was fantasy and adventure. The trapping made me akin to the creatures I pursued, part of the wilderness world to which they belonged. If anyone had accused me then of doing wrong to the animals I loved, I would not have understood. The magic of that boyhood world did not encompass understanding.

The weasel did not return, so I left the open water and started up the river. I had not gone more than a mile before I found the otter tracks. Two of them had been running and sliding over the smooth surface of the river for all the world like a couple of boys on clear ice. Otters love to play and in their traveling, wherever there is a chance, be it ice or snow or slippery mud, they indulge themselves.

I saw a family of them last summer on Robinson Lake in the Quetico just north of the border. We were trying to catch a pike off the cliff where the little creek from McIntyre comes down from the north. A little strip of sandy beach and a beaver house backed by a jungle of alder and willow and marsh grass: this was the setting. Although we were several hundred yards away when we first saw them, the violent splashing and diving off the beach told us what they were. In the wilds one can never mistake an otter group at play, their slipping in and out of the water, their seal-like antics.

On the chance of getting a better view, we paddled over to the beach and got out. In the wet sand we saw the tracks of the splayed, webbed feet that make the otter the swiftest-swimming mammal in the whole north country. Able to over-take a trout, they are as much at home in the water as on land. We got into the canoe again and paddled along the shore watching the great protruding shelves of rock, the granite boulders, the water itself, but not a sign of otters did we see. We decided that they must have gone back up the creek at the first flash of our paddles.

Then, just as we were rounding a rocky point with a flat surface jutting out over the water, we spotted three of them in full view rolling around and playing on the shelf. Surprised, we froze instantly and sat there within twenty feet of them, moving neither paddles nor eyes. The rock surface was covered with rough lichens, and the animals rolled upon it, stretched and scratched themselves, their bellies, their sides and backs. I could not help thinking of seals as I watched them, or sea otters—the smooth, almost boneless appearance of their bodies, the loose skins, the stiffly whiskered doglike faces. Never before in a lifetime of roaming the woods had I ever been so close.

The canoe drifted toward the rock, fifteen feet, ten, five, but not until the gunwale almost touched did they become aware. A moment of petrified realization, a swift plunge into the water, and they were gone. Then, to our amazement, they emerged on the other side of the canoe, treading water as only otters can, and looked us over boldly while they snorted and blew their nostrils clear. Up and down they bobbed like three anchored posts, at times seeming to emerge almost entirely out of the water. Then, their curiosity satisfied, they swam around the canoe and headed down along the shore the way they had come. A far larger head appeared out in the open lake—the mother otter blowing and whistling, warning her foolhardy young. We followed the family back to the beach, watching them diving and playing as though they had nothing to fear. They romped on the sand for a while and finally disappeared up the creek. *Lutra canadensis* is one of the most beautiful animals in the north and is blessed with the most spirit and personality.

Although a killer like its little cousin the ermine, it is somehow different. Surely, like the rest, it must kill to live, but when I see otters at play I feel that the killing must be almost incidental, that it is done in a spirit of play rather than to satisfy an implacable lust for blood.

Once I saw a mother otter with her young watching a tight little raft of half-grown mergansers coasting off the shore. They, too, were treading water, but I was not so close this time as I would have liked to be. I could see them plainly, however, and as yet they had not seen the canoe. Then the mother dove toward the unsuspecting raft of ducklings. A pause and one of them disappeared. A moment later she came ashore and gave the carcass to her young. Three different times this performance was repeated before the merganser took its little flock out of danger. To the otters life is never dull.

Toward midafternoon I saw the track of a lone fisher, *Martes pennanti*, the Pekan of the Indians. The track crossed the river and headed into a cedar swamp, and, had I been an Indian, I would have followed it, sure that eventually the animal would climb a tree. A trapper told me once that he had often stayed with a trail for days at a time and had almost always been successful. The fisher, too, is one of the *Mustelidæ*, but looks more like a stocky cat than the others, more like a small edition of the dreaded wolverine than the otter or the ermine. Equally at home in the trees or on the ground, it seems to prefer a range near running water. One of the few predators in the north able to kill a porcupine and live, it has learned to turn the animal over on its back or disembowel it in a tree. Its rarity in the north is perhaps one of the reasons why the porcupines are more numerous now than before.

With their chief enemy almost gone, there is no other here to fear.

I have seen only three live fishers in my life. Once just after the first snow came I saw one standing in plain view on a windfall not thirty feet away. In the dusk it looked black, though I knew its fur was grizzled tawny brown. It stood there and watched me and then slid off into the underbrush for all the world like a large cat on the prowl.

Once while exploring the rugged country between Robinson and Brent Lake I was resting on the edge of a cliff overlooking a rough talus slope below me. As I sat there above the valley I heard a sound, a scratching on the bark. Thinking it might be a red squirrel, I looked up, and there, crouched on a branch of a gnarled Norway pine not ten feet above, were two fishers watching me. I did not move, nor did they, and we sat there for some time staring at each other. Then, without warning, the animals leaped recklessly over the cliff to the jagged talus slope below. I was horrified, thinking that surely they would cripple themselves, but they bounded down unhurt into the birch and aspen of the valley. Only fishers could have done what they did then, only animals with perfect balance and control.

I have a strong attachment for all of the *Mustelidæ*, from the tiny ermine to the wolverine. Each is different, each a distinct personality. To be sure, the ecological factors are important— the endless cycle of carnivores and herbivores, the inevitable assimilation of vegetable matter to flesh and blood and back again. Part of the ancient cycle, one form of life cannot exist

without the other, but what really counts is how they make
me feel and how they contribute to the character and quality
of wilderness. They are an integral part of the wild, like all
the predators, but to me they somehow seem to belong to the
beginnings of things when the world was very young and the
wilderness was unchanged.

As I headed back through the woods, the west was flaming
and I saw the glow of it through the trees. From a hilltop I
could look across miles of purple ridges. The glow deepened
to lavender and then to mauve, and in between were streaks
of orange and apple green. I stood there on the hill and
watched until the cold reminded me to move. The temperature was dropping fast and I could feel the swift change as I
stood there. It would be twenty or thirty below by morning.
Perhaps the riffle down by the river would close now and
there would be no sight or sound of movement the next time
I came through.

CHAPTER 6

SKYLINE TRAIL

THIS afternoon we will take the Skyline Trail, the trail that more than any other gives us a feeling of distance and space. Vistas of wilderness will be ours, frozen swamps and lakes and ridges and winding trails through the woods. Along that trail toward sunset the light effects are more striking than anywhere else, for here the whole country lies before us.

Each day the trail is different, for the winds have their way with it and sculpture the drifts and tracks of the skis, and when the snow is dry and powdery as the sand of a dune, it is never the same from one moment to the next. Before us the trail is almost obliterated and only in the most protected spots is there any sign of travel. Here it is always new, never gets set and ridged as down in the valley, each day as fresh as though newly broken in, shifting every moment except when the sun is high. For a short time at noon the granular texture of the snow is softened and, in melting, holds itself together; but as soon as the sun's rays begin to slant, there is a rustling and whispering across the ridges, a piling up against the ski tracks, a remaking and rebuilding of each little drift.

We leave the high, bare slopes with their shifting snows and glide down into the close intimacy of birch and spruce, the trail winding in and out of thickets, down little slopes and up again, dodging under branches and around rocks and trees with the same feeling that portages give, or game trails, or any primitive paths through unbroken country. Cross-country skiing holds much of surprise and change, but best of all is the feeling of closeness to the woods themselves, to the sounds of birds and trees and the wind.

We cross a little field with a swift downhill run around the log haybarn of a settler, come out onto a long, undulating slope, then down into a rugged little valley where the cliffs are close, a climb to the top of a steep ridge, another swoop and climb, and then we are on the summit of a great ridge from which we can see across the ice of a sprawling lake. Beyond are many ridges and, twenty miles away, the scar of a great mining camp where men burrow the rock for iron ore, from the crest of that range fifty miles to the rocky coast of Lake Superior. This is the view we have come for. Here is the top of the Skyline Trail.

Below us are a spruce swamp and a long, winding hill. We push on our sticks and in an instant pick up speed. The snow has a silky feel to it now, and we weave and sway around the turns and know the floating lightness of dancers in ballet. Down through birch and aspen close enough to touch, around a pine in a swirl of snow, and suddenly we are in the quiet and deep green of the spruces.

It is dark and mysterious here after the high country, and tracks of rabbits crisscross the trail, even the deep trails of deer. There is little food here except along the fringes of the stand, but there is shelter from the winds and almost a warmth in its depths. The trees are slender and tall, but I know how old they are, for I counted the growth rings long ago, and in among them is the ancient sense of gloom and timelessness, of beginnings and endings, which all swamps seem to have.

Suddenly we burst out of the darkness and are skiing over the ice of the muskeg-bordered lake we saw from the ridge. The snow is hard here in the open, and we skate along the winding channels and between the encroaching banks of sphagnum. It is a temptation to follow the full length of the lake and soar down the clear surfaces where in the fall we flushed mallards and picked cranberries from the cushioned hummocks of moss, but the sun is sinking and we must cross the spruce swamp once more and climb to the top of the long slope before we can head for home.

It is much darker as we hurry through the spruces, and as we climb the hill down which we sped so swiftly a short time ago long shadows reach across the trail. At the top we stop to rest, turning to admire the herringbone pattern of our tracks and the lights playing across them. The west is in full glow and there are streamers of apple green and long splashes of orange and rose. A clump of birch is laced with molten silver. The mass of the swamp is changing now from dark green to black and the sky to blood red. Some of the color is washing onto the lake, the glistening pink reaches turning to mauve as the edges draw their purple from the bog. Twinkling lights mark the mining camp, a cluster of icy blue against the dark massiveness of the range.

We turn reluctantly, and the trail and its long shadows unravel before us. As the cold settles down, the skis hiss on the powder snow. The trees seem closer now and much taller, and the tiny ribbon of the trail with its ski-pole markings on either side disappears among them. A clump of brown cones in the very top of a tall pine suddenly bursts into flaming copper from a last ray of light, then suddenly it is brushed with black.

We are out of the timber at last and gliding down the crest of a winding esker smooth as a railroad grade. To one side is a tiny bog of sphagnum, perfectly round and nestled in a curve of the embankment. It was once the resting-place of a huge block of glacial ice, whose melting formed a pool. In time sphagnum covered it and trees grew around its edges. The mat is still resilient, and in the summer, when the bog is thawed, one can take long, springy steps across it. The rose of the pitcher plant is there with its strange clusters of insectivorous leaves, and in the spring there are swamp laurel and the waxy pale cups of Labrador tea. At dusk, when the plaintive note of the whitethroat sounds, you can smell its cold, sharp pungence.

In the early days a logging road ran down the top of the esker, a roadbed as perfect as though engineers had laid it out, with smooth shoulders, easy grades, and gentle curves. This serpentine ridge winding through the woods was once the bed of a glacial river beneath the ice; along its course plunged a frozen flood and uncounted tons of sediment and rocks. Above us was once a domed ceiling of crystalline blue. Ten thousand years or more have passed since the esker was formed; generations of forests have come and gone; fires have swept across it. It was an ancient roadway of the wild before the building of the pyramids.

An owl is hooting in the darkening timber, and over the trees hangs a thin sliver of a moon. It is time to go, and we drift easily down the old river bed. On the last long slope we gather speed and know the thrill all skiers have at night of seeming airborne, of floating down into the darkness of a bowl. For a fleeting instant we are part of that glacial river churning through its tunnel of ice, part of the milky-white water speeding toward the boulder-strewn outwash below.

Then out of the blackness and across an open field, and before us are the twinkling lights of town, the white lights of streets, the red neon lights of stores, a hazy Christmas-tree jumble of them in the dark pool of night below. A warm rosy haze overlies the town, and near that glow is home.

Down the last long slope our skis fairly sing. We weave and dip and shift our weight around the turns and stop in a flurry of snow as we turn toward the house. In a little while we are in the yard, unstrapping our skis. We stand them against the wall, plunge our poles into a drift, and stamp off the snow. For a while we have skied along the rim of the world and have known such things as dwellers in the town below have hardly dreamed about. We have known again the shifting snows of the high country, the winding trails through the valleys on the way to the great ridge, have known the glooms of the big bog, and have watched a sunset stain the snow of the lake. We have listened to the roar of a glacial river and been part of its wild plunging through the ice. We have looked across many miles of frozen wilderness and seen the sliver of a new moon in the purple of the west.

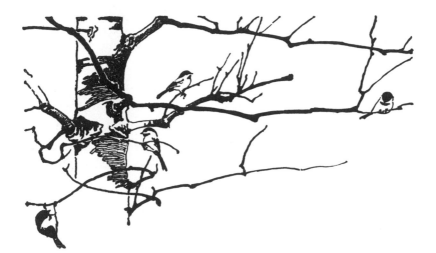

CHAPTER 7

BIRDS OF THE SKI TRAILS

T HE stars were still out, but along the top of the ridge was a faint blush of rose. As we slipped on our skis and fussed with the bindings, the blush deepened perceptibly and in its center was a touch of gold. The trails would be fast—none of the sandy dryness of sub-zero weather; with the coming of the sun, the skis would fly

231

and on the warm sides of trees the birds would be out feeding.

There is a sense of adventure and aliveness about the hour of dawn. Trees are more sharply etched, horizons more distinct, sensations more vivid than at any other time of day. In half an hour the sun would burst over the top of the hill, and if we were to be there to meet it, we would have to move.

Down the slope we sped, across the meadow into a thicket of alder, and up the long climb toward the top of the ridge. As we approached, frosted grasses began to glow with the exploring rays of the sun, first with a soft and mellow light and then with sparkling silver against the blue of the sky. At the crest we stopped and leaned on our sticks, panting and blowing from the climb. The east was now aflame, its center a caldron of burning gold. As the sun burst over the horizon, we stared as though we had never seen it before, as though the grand display had been planned for us alone. The blues and frosty purples were brushed away and daylight lay over the wilderness before us.

As we rested there, a flock of snow buntings drifted across the open field behind us, came close enough so we could hear their twittering and see the white flash of wings and fawn-marked sides and backs. How soft their flight and their careening swoop as they dashed into a patch of weeds, scattering the seeds over the snow, then swung back and settled as gently as the flakes for which they are named.

We pushed on our sticks, gathered speed on the east slope, wove in and out of a stand of white birch now blazing in the first sunlight. A sharp turn and another dip and suddenly we were in an open space with a tiny bog in its very center. It was there we saw the Bohemian waxwings. Larger by far than their lesser cousins of the summer months, they showed the same sleekness, the jaunty topknots, the yellow tips to the tails. They were feeding on the red berries of a mountain ash and the snow was red with the skins and juicy pulps. Down from the wilds of the far northwest, in a short time they would be gone, either back to where they had come from or south on the trail of berries and seeds. True Bohemians, they knew better than many species the secret of freedom, moving when and where they chose without seeming to depend on the dictates of their hormones. As though reading my thoughts, they took to the air and flew straight into the sun. The little ash was stripped clean and they were off on the search for more.

Just ahead the trail led into a stand of birch and aspen. Here the snow was deep and we stopped to rest from the labor of breaking trail. While we were leaning on our sticks, a ruffed grouse bounced out of the snow, flew into the top of a birch, and began budding as unconcernedly as though it had never been disturbed. Two more came out so close we might have touched them with our poles, one of them hurtling over the ridge, the other flying back into the protection of the balsams. We could see where they had walked through a clump of sumac, the careful pattern of tracks winding in and out of the bushes as they fed on the rosy clumps of seeds. Wing marks showed where they had flown into the trees before dropping to their cozy nests in the fresh, unbroken snow.

233

It was good to see them and to know there were still a few survivors after the hunting-season and the disease cycle that decimated their numbers to near-extinction every few years. There just had to be a few so that during the warm days of May their drumming would sound from the ridges, and that in the fall they could startle us on the logging roads and we could watch their wild, twisting flight through the trees.

We crossed an alder-grown valley and soon were skiing up an old tote road once known as the Indian Trail. On the highlands were red and white pine, and here for the first time we heard the soft nasal twang of the rose-breasted nuthatches and caught a glimpse of them high in the tops, scurrying about, exploring the branches in the new warmth of the sun. Here, too, we saw the chickadees darting about the sun-drenched masses of boughs and heard all through those tops the cheeriest music in the north: *chickadee-dee-dee-deeeee*.

When I gave the mating-call, the lonely double note so common in the days of spring, a curious blackcap left the sunshine and dashed around and around us, looking for the bird foolish enough to give that call in the dead of winter. The little bird was fluffed against the cold, and never for an instant was it still; it soon abandoned its search and flew back to the warmth and music of the pine tops.

Leaving the Indian Trail, we headed south toward the hills overlooking Moss Lake. Here was open country, smooth glaciated ridges with scattered clumps of pine and balsam reminding us of the park-like expanses of high country near timber line. Around us now were the soft, melodious warblings of evening grosbeaks. A flock of them drifted by and settled in a clump of ash. Soft gold they were, with dashes of black and white, the same birds that had robbed us of uncounted pounds of sunflower seeds since the first coming of the snow.

When we reached the top of the ridge overlooking the lake we stopped again to rest and listen. No sound now of nuthatches or chickadees, no warbling of grosbeaks—just the deep silence of great expanses of winter landscape. Down below us was a swamp with the dark pinnacles of massed spruce extending from the base of the ridge to the edge of the bog surrounding a narrow, winding lake. Across the lake were ridge after ridge of spruce and pine, aspen and birch and balsam, and beyond them the deep-blue horizons of the Giants Range.

Then we heard a sound we had not expected to hear in broad daylight: the call of the great horned owl, and then an answering call much deeper and more resonant than the first. Back and forth went the booming—*Hoo-hooo-hoo-hooooooooo*—and with it the fear of death came to the cowering snowshoe rabbits down in the alders, to squirrels and mice, to the budding partridge back in the birches, to countless creatures for miles around. One of the most feared of hunting-calls in the north, that sound brought visions of lonely valleys bathed in moonlight, of rivers and lakes and campsites at dusk. No wonder the wilderness lay frozen and still, no wonder the warbling had stopped.

As we came out of the spruce we circled the edge of the swamp and saw before us a crooked ash laden with great bunches of brown and withered seeds leaning far out over the sphagnum. There was aliveness and color in that tree—the flashing rose and gray of the pine grosbeaks. As we neared, we saw that the tree was full of them, the males resplendent with the color combination that to us has no equal in the north. So conscious were we of its beauty that we were always on the lookout, no matter where we happened to be. During the fall there had been a sumac outlined in frostbitten crimson against a lichen-covered ledge, then a scarlet woodbine encircling a silvery stub, and a rose-colored maple standing all alone in a mass of gray boulders on the Nina Moose.

Several males flew down to the snow to pick up the seeds that had fallen, and there we really had a chance to admire them. When they saw us, their music stopped and they flew to a clump of pine across the lake. We watched them until they were out of sight, then continued along the shore. The hillsides were not somber any more. There was color in among them.

We skied over the ice toward a little island grown thickly with tamarack and black spruce. All the way across we heard the staccato beat of the Cock of the Woods, the pileated woodpecker, and saw its undulating flight from a dead tamarack on the island to the top of a distant ridge on the north shore.

Circling back into the woods toward home, we stopped in a sunny opening to boil a pot of tea and eat the sandwiches we had brought. As expected, we became hosts to a pair of whisky-jacks who drifted into our lunch spot without a sound.

Dr. John Bigsby noticed them on a border expedition in 1823 and wrote in his diary: "We were visited by two of the birds called Whistling John. It has a long bill and is almost all feathers. Its back is brown and breast white. It is extremely familiar and goes about whistling a little note of its own, seeking small objects which it hoards. It is the size of an English blackbird."

While a little off on the birds' color, Dr. Bigsby must have noticed as we did the way they drifted in, their strange ventriloquism, and the muted warbling that seemed to come from everywhere at once. We tossed out bits of bread, and gradually they became so bold that they took them within reach of our hands. Whisky-jacks, whistling johns, Canada jays, camp robbers—what a place they have made for themselves in the bush country of the Canadian Shield!

Going back through the woods, we saw a raven circling high overhead and knew it was watching our progress over the trail as a flock of them had watched me years ago when I was traveling over the rotting ice of New Found Lake to the east. They had warned me that day, for ravens know where the ice is bad and the hunting good. This time we were safe, for there was no ice to cross, and the bird soared and soared high in the blue without even coming close.

As the sun began to slant, the warbling and twittering stopped. The cold descended and purple shadows reached out from the timber. By four thirty the hollows were deep in dusk, and in the west the dark trunks of pine and spruce were backed by golden light. As we topped the ridge above home, the sun was trembling on the western horizon; then it sank as swiftly into the frosty blue as it had emerged nine hours before. A last look at the flaming sky and we sped down into the valley we had left at dawn.

CHAPTER 8

TIMBER WOLVES

I COULD hear them plainly now on both sides of the river, could hear the brush crack as they hurdled windfalls in their path. Once I thought I saw one, a drifting gray shadow against the snow, but it was only a branch swaying in the light of the moon. When I heard the full-throated bawling howl, I should have had chills racing up and down my spine. Instead, I was thrilled to know that the big grays might have picked up my trail and were following me down the glistening frozen highway of the river.

It was a beautiful night for travel—twenty below, and the only sound the steady swish and creak of my snowshoes on the crust. There was a great satisfaction in knowing that the wolves were in the country, that it was wild enough and still big enough for them to roam and hunt. That night the wilderness of the Quetico-Superior was what the voyageurs had known two hundred years before, as primitive and unchanged as before discovery.

Some months before, I had had the same kind of experience on a pack trip in the Sun River country of Montana. In the bottom of a canyon I saw the fresh track of a big grizzly in the soft muck beside a glacial creek. Although I did not see the bear, I knew it was near by. Those tracks changed the country immediately for me. From that moment on, it was the land of Lewis and Clark, the land of the mountain men of the last century, a valley of the old west.

The river ahead narrowed down to where two points of timber came out from either bank, and as I approached, I sensed instinctively the possibilities of attack. I was familiar with the wolf lore of the Old World, the packs on the steppes of Russia, the invasion of farms and villages, and had I believed the lurid tales of our early settlers and explorers, I might have been afraid. To the best of my knowledge, however, including the files of the U.S. Fish and Wildlife Service, for the past twenty-five years there has never been a single authenticated instance of unprovoked attack on man.

But still there was a feeling of uneasiness and apprehension, and I knew that if the animals were concerned with anything but satisfying their curiosity, the narrows would be the place for a kill. A swift rush from both points at the same time, a short, unequal scuffle in the snow, and it would be all over. My bones would go down with the ice in the spring, and no one would ever hear the story and no one would be able to explain.

As I neared the points of spruce, I could almost hear the crash of heavy bodies against windfalls and brush. Weighing a hundred, even as much as a hundred and twelve pounds or more, timber wolves are huge and powerful, can bring down a caribou or a moose, have nothing to fear on the entire continent but man. This was not the first time I had felt they were playing their game of hide-and-seek with me. On other lone midwinter expeditions I had sensed that they were close—a hunch perhaps, but as instinctive a reaction when in their immediate range as though I had actually seen them. I knew, as I hiked along that night, that I was being watched, a lone dark spot moving slowly along the frozen river.

That very morning I had seen where they had pulled down an old buck on the ice of a little lake, seen how they had run the deer to exhaustion and then sliced at his hamstrings, his flanks, and his throat, seen the long crimson spurt where they had ripped the jugular, seen the bits of mangled hide on the snow. He had been large and his horns were broad and palmate, but in the trampled bloody circle where he had made his last stand, he had not lasted long. He might have died slowly of starvation or disease, but he died as he should when his time had come, fighting for his life against his age-old enemies, dying like the valiant warrior he was out on the open ice.

The wolves had not eaten much, only the entrails and the viscera, but they would return, I knew, to satisfy themselves again. Such was the habit of their kind until we interfered with poison and trap and taught them caution and fear. When that happened, they learned to leave the carcasses after the first feeding and killed more than they would have normally. That kill was part of the age-old cycle of dependency between the wolves and the deer. The predators, by the elimination of the old, the weak, and the diseased, improved the character of the herd and kept the younger and more virile breeding-stock alert and aware of danger. The deer provided food when there was no other source, when the heavy snows hid small rodents, the fish and snakes, grubs and berries and birds that gave the wolves sustenance during all other seasons of the year. There on the ice was evidence of the completed cycle, and, though all kills are gruesome things, I was glad to see it, for it meant a wilderness in balance, a primitive country that as yet had not been tamed.

In the narrows the spruces stood tall and black against the sky. The shores there were only a stone's throw apart. I must walk straight down the center, must not run, must not break my pace; and suddenly I was aware that, in spite of reason and my knowledge of the predators, ancient reactions were coming to the fore, intuitive warnings out of the past. In spite of what I knew, I was responding to the imagined threat of the narrows like a stone-age hunter cut off from his cave.

Then, far ahead, way beyond the dangerous points, two shadows broke from cover and headed directly down the river toward me. I stopped, slipped off my pack, and waited. Nearer and nearer they came, running with the easy, loose-jointed grace that only the big timber wolves seem to have. A hundred yards away they stopped and tried to get my wind; they wove back and forth, swaying as they ran. Then, about fifty feet away they stopped and looked me over. In the moonlight their gray hides glistened and I could see the greenish glint of their eyes. Not a movement or a sound. We stood watching each other as though such meetings were expected and common-place.

As suddenly as they had appeared, they whirled and were off down the river, two drifting forms against the ice. Never before had I been that close, possibly never again would I see the glint in timber wolves' eyes or have such a chance to study their free and fluid movement. Once more came the long howl, this time far back from the river, and then I heard them no more.

A little later I pushed open the door of the little cabin and touched a match to the waiting tinder in the stove. As I sat there listening to the roar of it and stowing away my gear, I realized fully what I had seen and what I had felt. Had it not been twenty below, I would have left the door opened wide so as not to lose the spell of the moonlit river and the pack ranging its shores.

After I was warmed through and had eaten my supper, I

stepped outside once more. The river was still aglisten, and the far shore looked black and somber. An owl hooted back in the spruce, and I knew what that meant in the moonlit glades. A tree cracked sharply with the frost, and then it was still, so still that I could hear the beating of my heart. At last I caught what I was listening for—the long-drawn quavering howl from over the hills, a sound as wild and indigenous to the north as the muskegs or the northern lights. That was wilderness music, something as free and untamed as there is on this earth.

Although thrilled to hear them once again, I was saddened when I thought of the constant war of extermination which goes on all over the continent. Practically gone from the United States, wolves are now common only in the Quetico-Superior country, in Canada, and in Alaska, and I knew the day might come when, because of man's ignorance, the great grays would be gone even from there. Just before leaving on my trip up the river I had seen a news story about the killing of six timber wolves by airplane hunters in the Rainy Lake country. The picture showed them strung up on the wing of the plane and the hunters proudly posed beside them. As I studied that picture and the applauding captions, I wondered if the day would ever come when we would understand the importance of wolves.

Knowing the nature of our traditions of the old frontier and the pioneer complex that still guides our attitudes toward wildlife, I realized that it might never come. We still do not realize that today we can enjoy the wilderness without fear, still do not appreciate the part that predators play in the balanced ecology of any natural community. We seem to prefer herds of semi-domesticated deer and elk and moose, swarms of small game with their natural alertness gone. It is as though we were interested in conserving only a meat supply and nothing of the semblance of the wild.

It was cold, bitterly cold, and I hurried back into the cabin and crawled into my sleeping-bag in the corner bunk. Beside me was my pack and in a pocket my brush-worn copy of Thoreau. I took it out, thumbed through it by the light of the candle.

"We need," he said, "to witness our own limits transgressed and some life pasturing freely where we never wander."

SIGURD F. OLSON (1899–1982) was one of the greatest environmentalists of the twentieth century. A conservation activist and popular writer, Olson introduced a generation of Americans to the importance of wilderness. He served as President of the Wilderness Society and the National Parks Association, and as a consultant to the federal government on wilderness preservation and ecological problems. He earned many honors, including the highest possible from the Sierra Club, National Wildlife Federation, and Izaak Walton League.

Olson's books include *The Singing Wilderness* (1956), *Listening Point* (1958), *The Lonely Land* (1961), *Runes of the North* (1963), *Open Horizons* (1969), *The Hidden Forest* (1969), *Wilderness Days* (1972), *Reflections from the North Country* (1976), and *Of Time and Place* (1982). His books created a new genre of nature writing that was infused with beauty and respect for our nation's wild places. He was a recipient of the John Burroughs Medal, the highest honor in nature writing, and frequently appeared on bestseller lists across the nation.

Olson lived and worked in Ely, Minnesota, gateway to the Quetico-Superior region, for most of his life.